Introduction

As parents and educators, we recognize the pivotal role mathematics plays in shaping a child's academic journey and future success. Yet, the path to mathematical proficiency can often seem daunting, fraught with challenges and complexities. That's where the transformative power of MathFlare Workbooks shine through, illuminating the way forward with clarity, precision, and purpose.

Introducing MathFlare Workbooks – a beacon of guidance, a testament to excellence, and a catalyst for achievement. Crafted with meticulous care and expertise, MathFlare Workbooks stand as paragons of educational excellence, designed to nurture young minds, ignite a passion for learning, and develop a deep-rooted understanding of mathematical concepts.

Picture this: your child eagerly delves into the pages of Mathflare Workbook, greeted by a step-by-step guide illuminated with vivid examples that demystify complex mathematical concepts. With each turn of the page, they embark on a journey of discovery, encountering thoughtfully curated practice questions that reinforce learning and hone problem-solving skills. And when they unveil the answers to those very questions, a sense of accomplishment blossoms within them – a tangible reward for their hard work and dedication.

But MathFlare Workbooks are more than just tools for learning; they are pathways to comprehension, fostering a deep-seated understanding of mathematical concepts through a sequential, logical flow. From fundamental principles to advanced problem-solving strategies, every chapter builds upon the last, ensuring a robust foundation upon which future knowledge can be constructed.

As parents, we yearn for nothing more than to see our children thrive, to witness the spark of inspiration ignited within them as they conquer academic challenges with confidence and poise. MathFlare Workbooks serve as partners in this noble endeavor, offering not just practice questions, but the keys to unlocking a world of opportunity.

And for teachers, MathFlare Workbooks stand as invaluable allies in the quest to cultivate mathematical proficiency in the classroom. With answers readily available, instructors can focus on guiding and nurturing their students, confident in the knowledge that MathFlare Workbooks provide a solid framework upon which to build.

In the pages of MathFlare Workbooks, we find not just the promise of academic excellence, but the seeds of a brighter tomorrow. So let us embrace the power of mathematics, let us champion the journey of learning, and let us pave the way for a generation of young minds poised to shape the world. With MathFlare Workbooks as our guide, the possibilities are infinite, and the future, bright.

Table of Contents

MathFlare
MATH
WORKBOOK
5
Multiplication Division
Place Value and Expanded Notations
Fractions and Geometry
Unit Conversion
Step by Step Guide and Essential Practice with Answers
MathFlare Publishing

MathFlare
MATH
WORKBOOK
5-6
Multiplication Division
Place Value and Expanded Notations
Fractions and Geometry
Units and Statistics
Step by Step Guide and Essential Practice with Answers
MathFlare Publishing

MathFlare
MATH
WORKBOOK
6
Integers and Statistics
Arithmetic and Pre-Algebra
Fractions and Geometry
Ratio and Percentage
Step by Step Guide and Essential Practice with Answers
MathFlare Publishing

MathFlare
MATH
WORKBOOK
6-7
Arithmetic and Pre-Algebra
Ratio, Percent Proportion
Geometry
Statistics
Step by Step Guide and Essential Practice with Answers
MathFlare Publishing

MathFlare
MATH
WORKBOOK
7
Pre-Algebra
Ratio, Percent Proportion
Geometry
Statistics
Step by Step Guide and Essential Practice with Answers
MathFlare Publishing

MathFlare
MATH
WORKBOOK
7-8
Pre-Algebra
Ratio, Percent Proportion
Geometry and Cartesian Plane
Statistics
Step by Step Guide and Essential Practice with Answers
MathFlare Publishing

MathFlare
MATH
WORKBOOK
8-9
Pre-Algebra
Ratio, Proportion and Percentages
Linear Equations
Geometry and Cartesian Plane
Step by Step Guide and Essential Practice with Answers
MathFlare Publishing

MathFlare
MATH
WORKBOOK
8
Pre-Algebra
Percentage
Linear Equations
Geometry
Step by Step Guide and Essential Practice with Answers
MathFlare Publishing

Counting and Numbers

Skip Counting

Skip counting is a fun and useful skill that helps us count faster by jumping over some numbers. It's a valuable tool for developing number sense and fluency in mathematics.

Count by 1 from 1 to 100

1	2	3	4	5	6	7	8	9	10
11	12	13	14	15	16	17	18	19	20
21	22	23	24	25	26	27	28	29	30
31	32	33	34	35	36	37	38	39	40
41	42	43	44	45	46	47	48	49	50
51	52	53	54	55	56	57	58	59	60
61	62	63	64	65	66	67	68	69	70
71	72	73	74	75	76	77	78	79	80
81	82	83	84	85	86	87	88	89	90
91	92	93	94	95	96	97	98	99	100

<u>Counting Up</u>

Counting the numbers in ascending order or adding numbers in a sequence.

97	98	99	100	101	102	103	104	105	106

<u>Counting Down</u>

Counting the numbers in descending order or subtracting numbers in a sequence.

92	91	90	89	88	87	86	85	84	83

<u>Counting Patterns:</u>

It refers to sequences of numbers that follow a specific rule or pattern: such as counting by 2s and 3s, adding 2s and 3s in sequence.

<u>Count by 2s</u>

Count by 2 from 52 to 70

52	54	56	58	60	62	64	66	68	70

<u>Count by 3s</u>

Count by 3 from 72 to 99

72	75	78	81	84	87	90	93	96	99

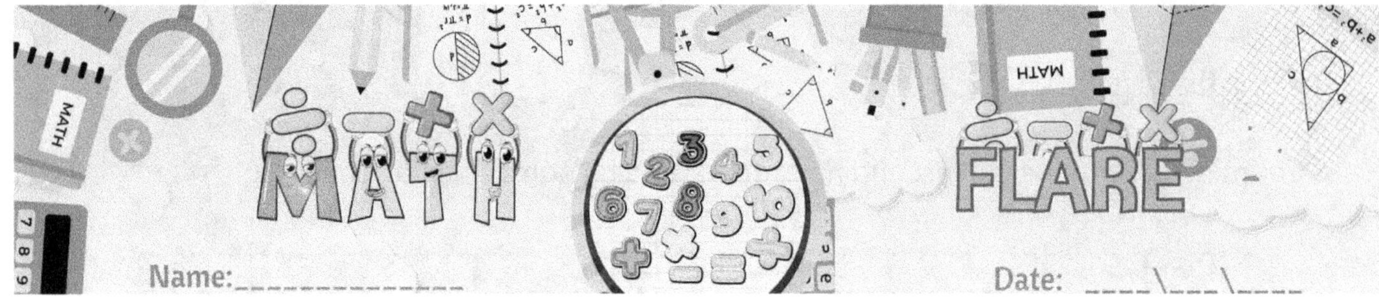

Skip Counting: Ascending

1. Count by 1 from 1 to 100

1									
					16	17			
					26		28	29	
		33							
		43		45					
								59	
		63				67	68		
71	72								
		83			86	87			
91			94						100

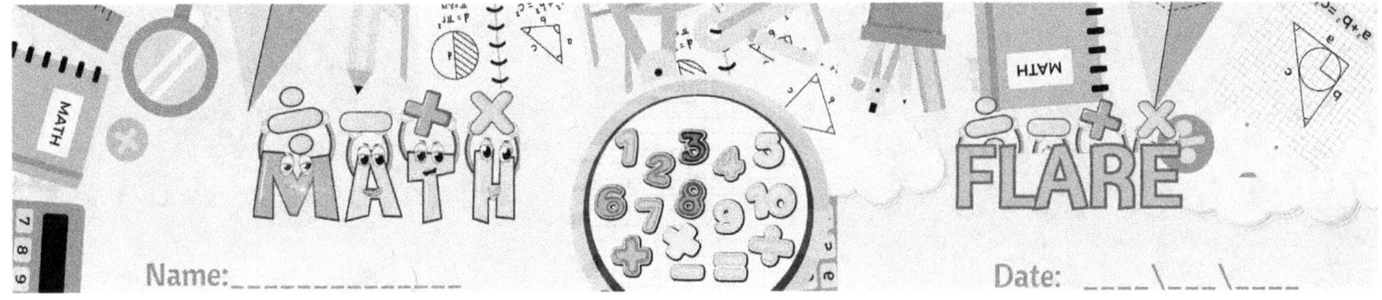

Skip Counting: Ascending

2. Count by 1 from 1 to 100

1									
								19	
		23							
31									
									50
	52								60
						67	68		
	82								
								99	100

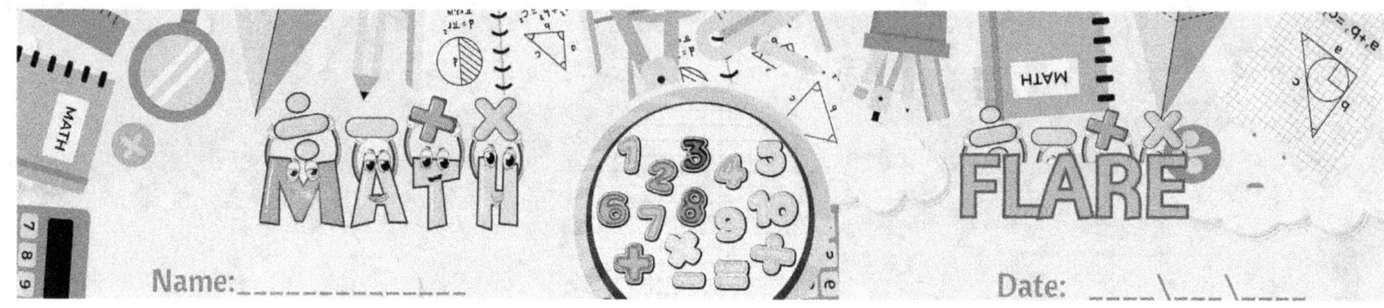

Skip Counting: Ascending

3. Count by 1 from 1 to 100

1									
								100	

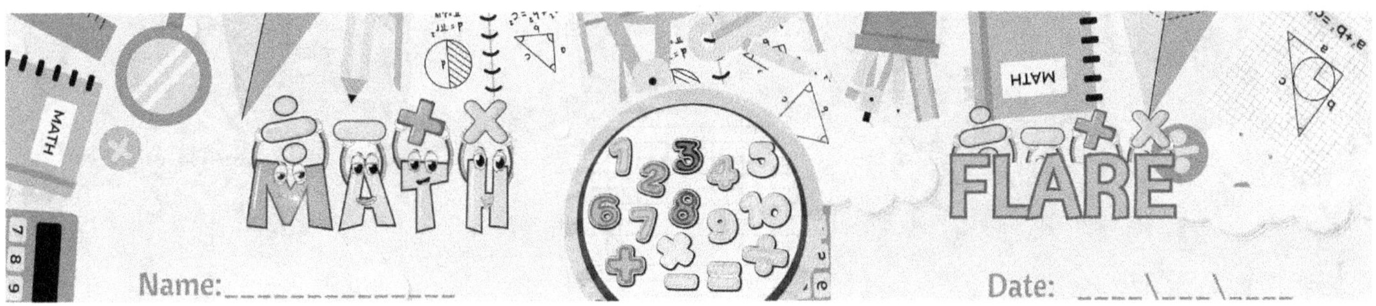

Count Up

Fill in the missing numbers by counting up.

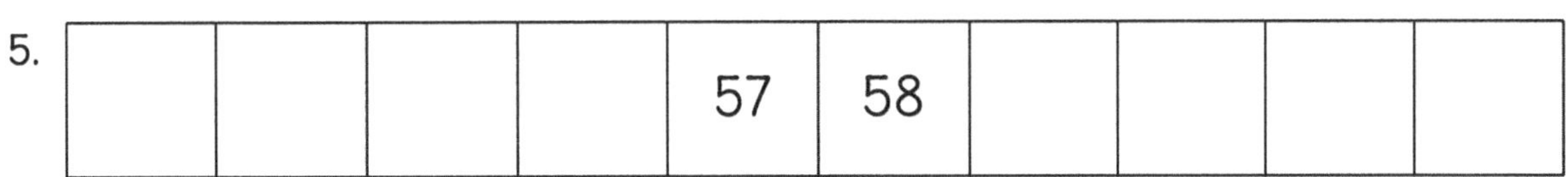

4. | | | | | | | 68 | 69 | | |

5. | | | | | 57 | 58 | | | | |

6. | 77 | 78 | | | | | | | | |

7. | | | | | | | 28 | 29 | | |

8. | | 40 | 41 | | | | | | | |

9. | | | 62 | 63 | | | | | | |

10. | | | | | 33 | 34 | | | | |

11. | | | | | 72 | 73 | | | | |

12. | | 99 | 100 | | | | | | | |

13. | 91 | 92 | | | | | | | | |

14. | | | | | 8 | 9 | | | | |

15. | | | | 61 | 62 | | | | | |

16. | | | | | | | 78 | 79 | | |

17. | | | | | 48 | 49 | | | | |
|---|---|---|---|---|---|---|---|---|---|

18. | | 101 | 102 | | | | | | | |
|---|---|---|---|---|---|---|---|---|---|

19. | | | | | 41 | 42 | | | | |
|---|---|---|---|---|---|---|---|---|---|

20. | | 29 | 30 | | | | | | | |
|---|---|---|---|---|---|---|---|---|---|

21. | 35 | 36 | | | | | | | | |
|---|---|---|---|---|---|---|---|---|---|

22. | 71 | 72 | | | | | | | | |
|---|---|---|---|---|---|---|---|---|---|

23. | 81 | 82 | | | | | | | | |
|---|---|---|---|---|---|---|---|---|---|

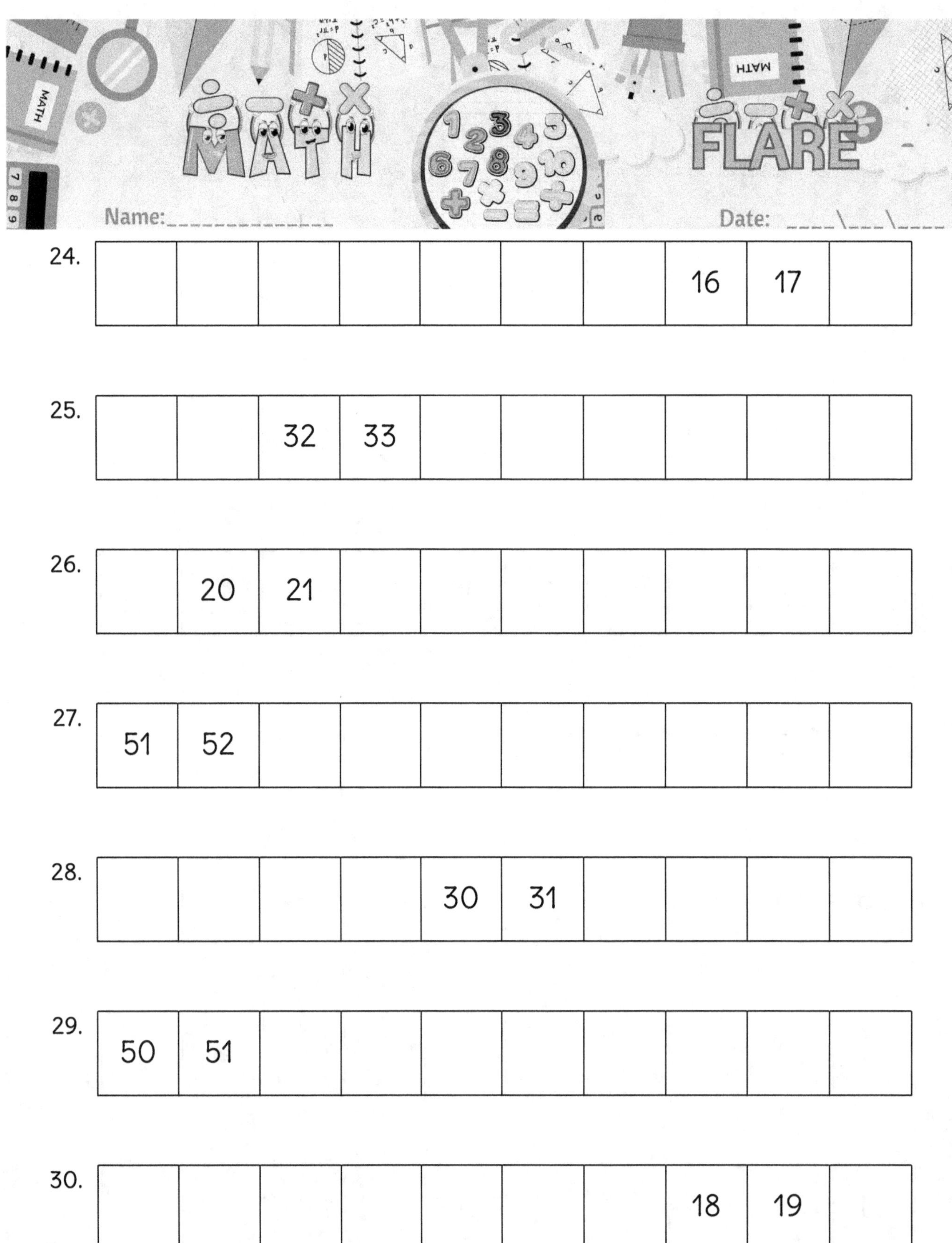

24.

| | | | | | | | 16 | 17 | |

25.

| | | 32 | 33 | | | | | | |

26.

| | 20 | 21 | | | | | | | |

27.

| 51 | 52 | | | | | | | | |

28.

| | | | | 30 | 31 | | | | |

29.

| 50 | 51 | | | | | | | | |

30.

| | | | | | | | 18 | 19 | |

31.

				21	22				

32.

						102	103		

33.

				13	14				

34.

				19	20				

35.

			73	74					

36.

	26	27							

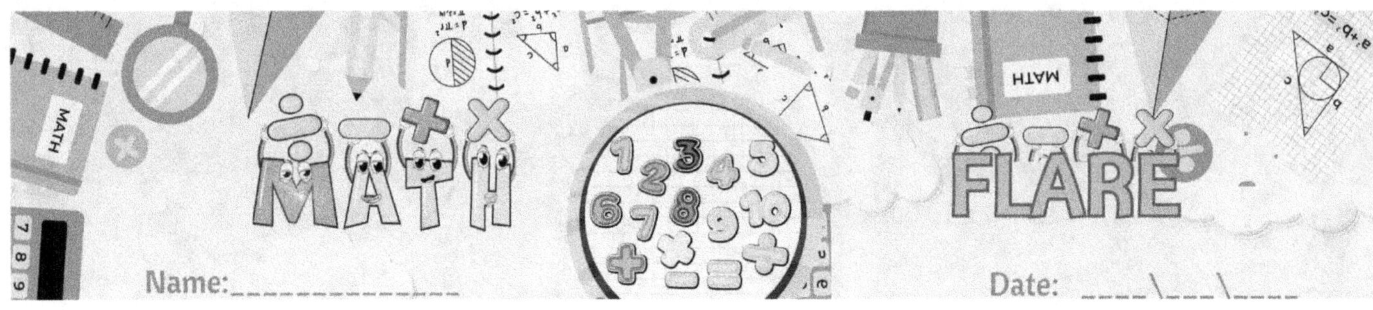

Count Down

Fill in the missing numbers by counting Down.

37. | | | | | 76 | 75 | | | | |
|---|---|---|---|---|---|---|---|---|---|

38. | | 17 | 16 | | | | | | | |
|---|---|---|---|---|---|---|---|---|---|

39. | | | 67 | 66 | | | | | | |
|---|---|---|---|---|---|---|---|---|---|

40. | | | | | | 34 | 33 | | | |
|---|---|---|---|---|---|---|---|---|---|

41. | | | 39 | 38 | | | | | | |
|---|---|---|---|---|---|---|---|---|---|

42. | | | | | | | | 6 | 5 | |
|---|---|---|---|---|---|---|---|---|---|

43. | | 43 | 42 | | | | | | |

44. | | 66 | 65 | | | | | | |

45. | | | | | | | 32 | 31 | | |

46. | | | 41 | 40 | | | | | | |

47. | | | 21 | 20 | | | | | | |

48. | | 56 | 55 | | | | | | |

49. | | | | | | 5 | 4 | | |

50.

						72	71		

51.

51	50								

52.

		62	61						

53.

30	29								

54.

							10	9	

55.

							82	81	

56.

	80	79							

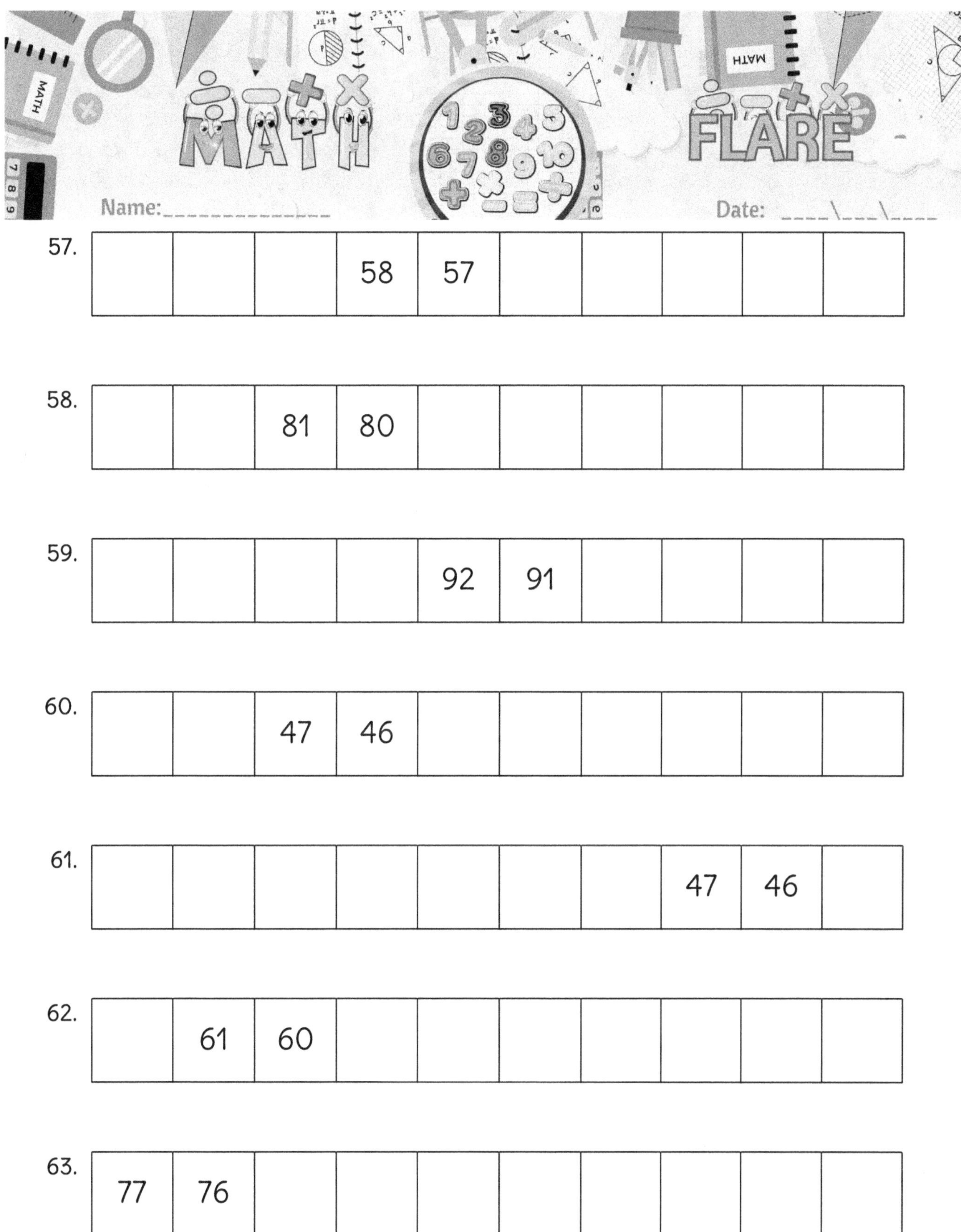

57.

			58	57					

58.

		81	80						

59.

				92	91				

60.

		47	46						

61.

							47	46	

62.

	61	60							

63.

77	76								

64. | | | | 50 | 49 | | | | | |

65. | 20 | 19 | | | | | | | | |

66. | | | | | 27 | 26 | | | | |

67. | | | | 10 | 9 | | | | | |

68. | | | 8 | 7 | | | | | | |

69. | | | | | | | | 43 | 42 | |

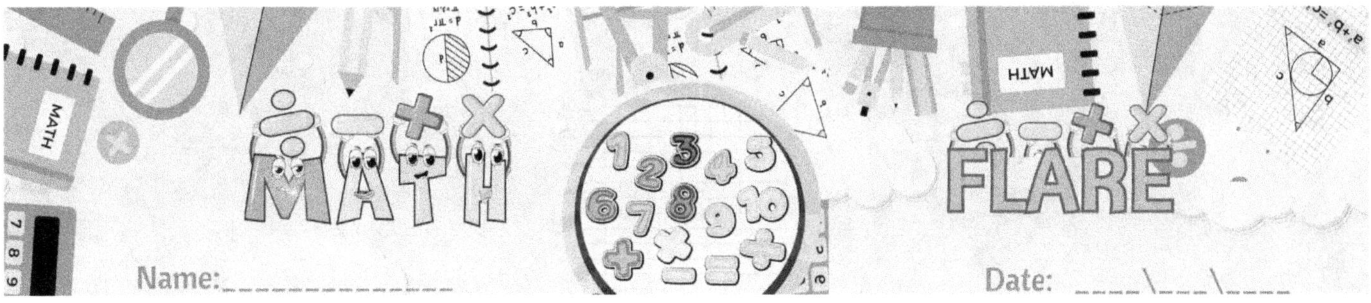

Count by 2s

Complete the counting tables.

70. Count by 2 from 91 to 109

	93								

71. Count by 2 from 87 to 105

87									

72. Count by 2 from 11 to 29

			17						

73. Count by 2 from 43 to 61

	45								

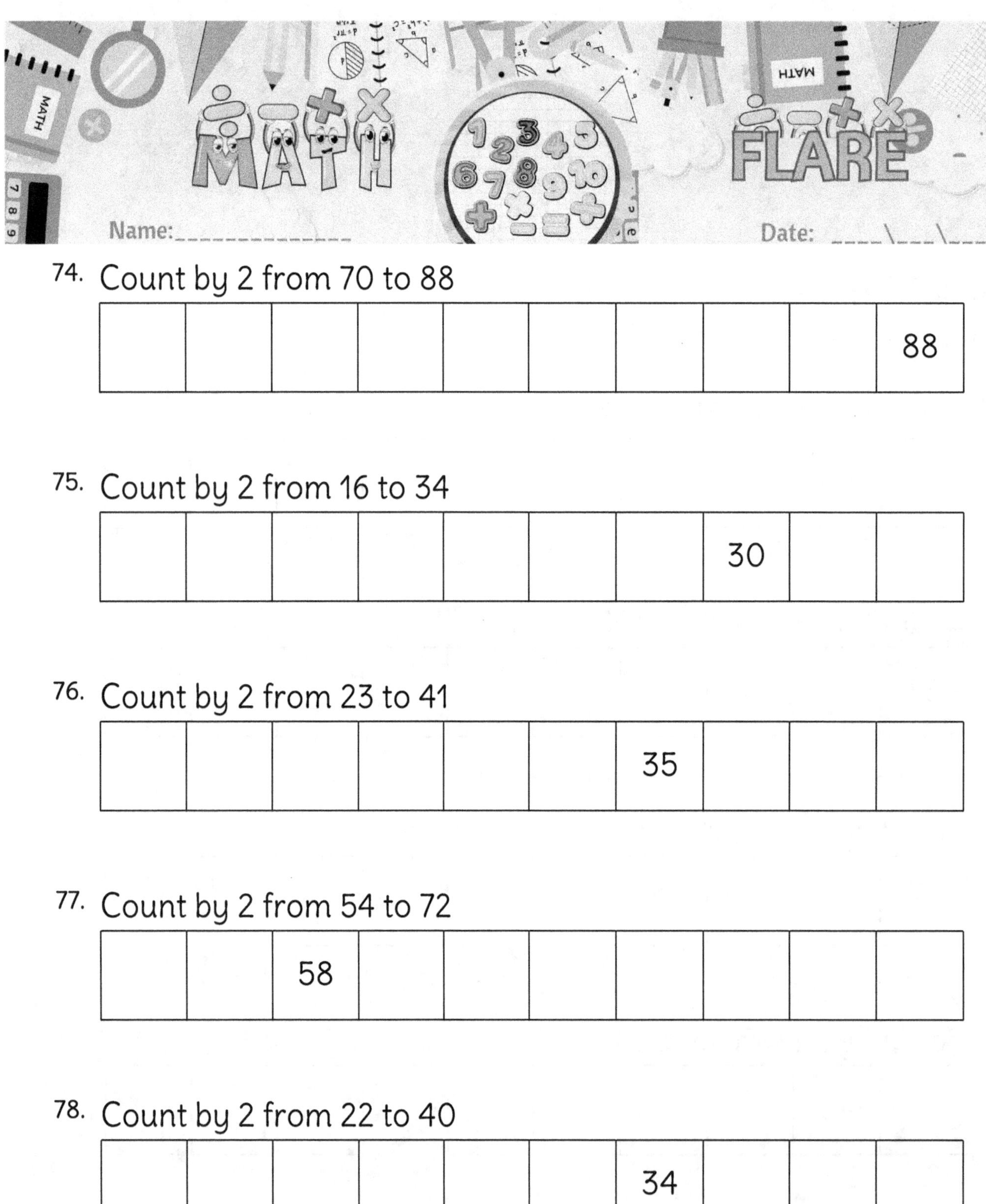

74. Count by 2 from 70 to 88

									88

75. Count by 2 from 16 to 34

							30		

76. Count by 2 from 23 to 41

						35			

77. Count by 2 from 54 to 72

		58							

78. Count by 2 from 22 to 40

						34			

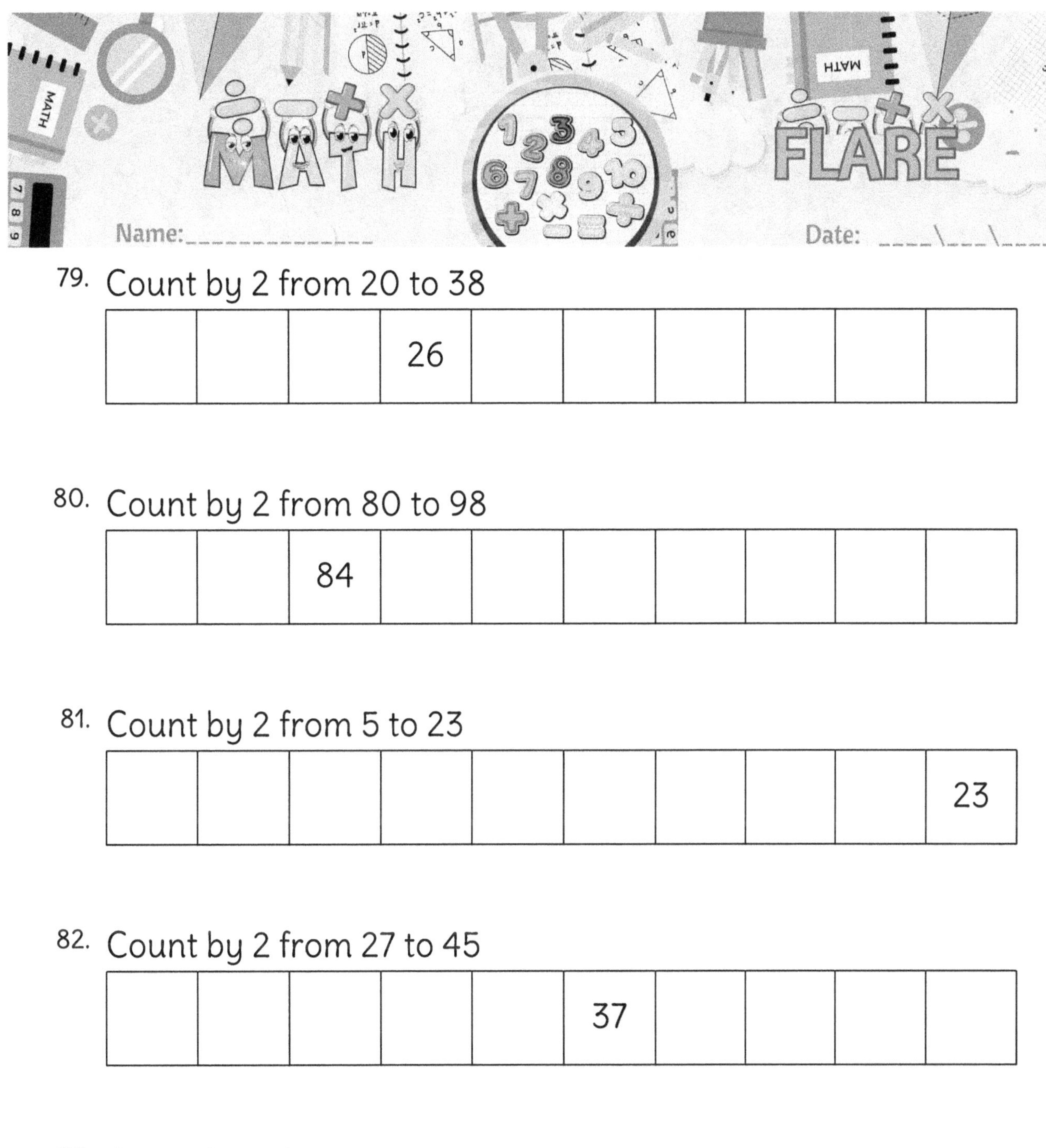

Name: _______________   Date: ____________

79. Count by 2 from 20 to 38

			26						

80. Count by 2 from 80 to 98

		84							

81. Count by 2 from 5 to 23

									23

82. Count by 2 from 27 to 45

				37					

83. Count by 2 from 42 to 60

						54			

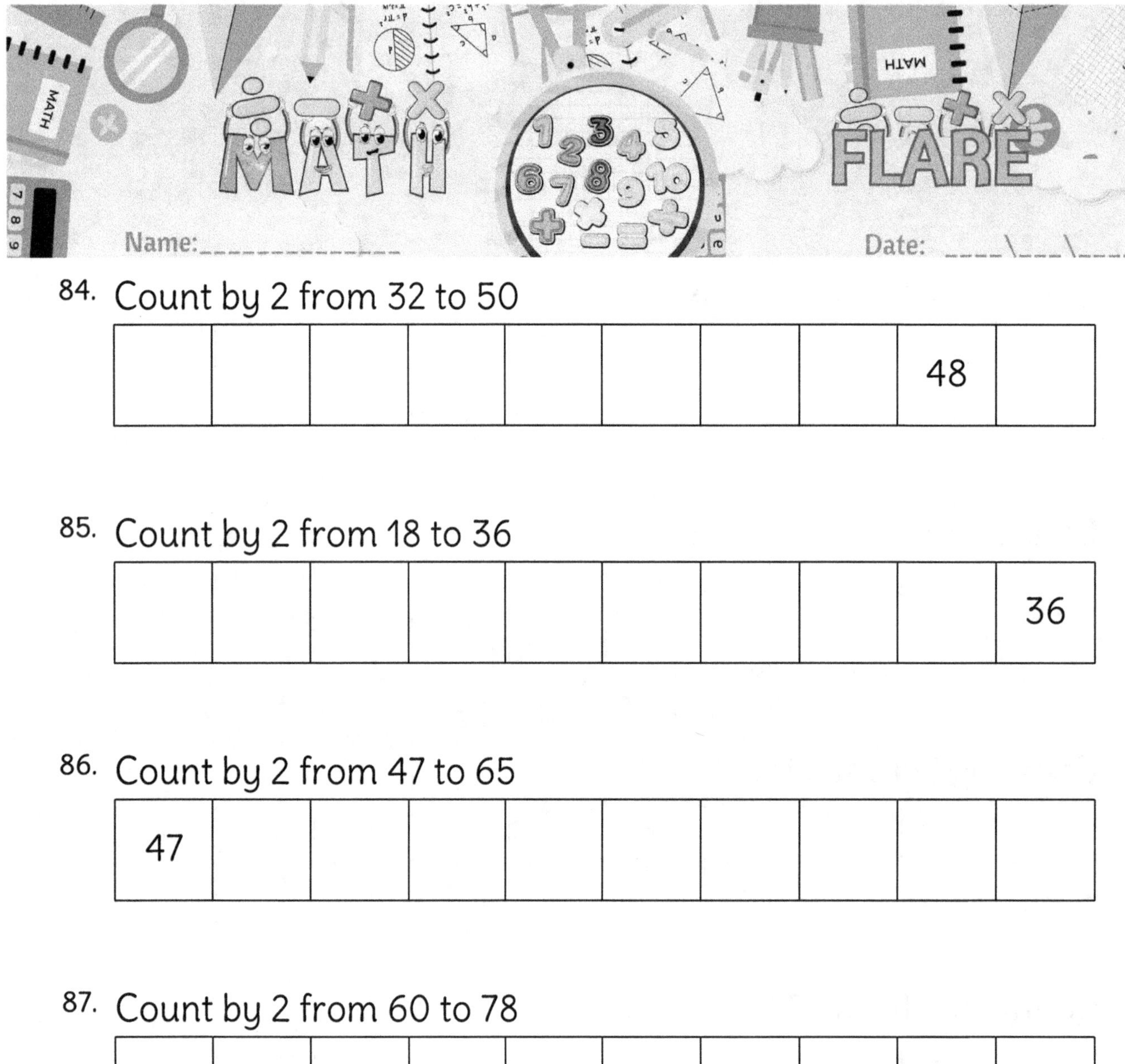

84. Count by 2 from 32 to 50

								48	

85. Count by 2 from 18 to 36

									36

86. Count by 2 from 47 to 65

47									

87. Count by 2 from 60 to 78

		64							

88. Count by 2 from 96 to 114

				106					

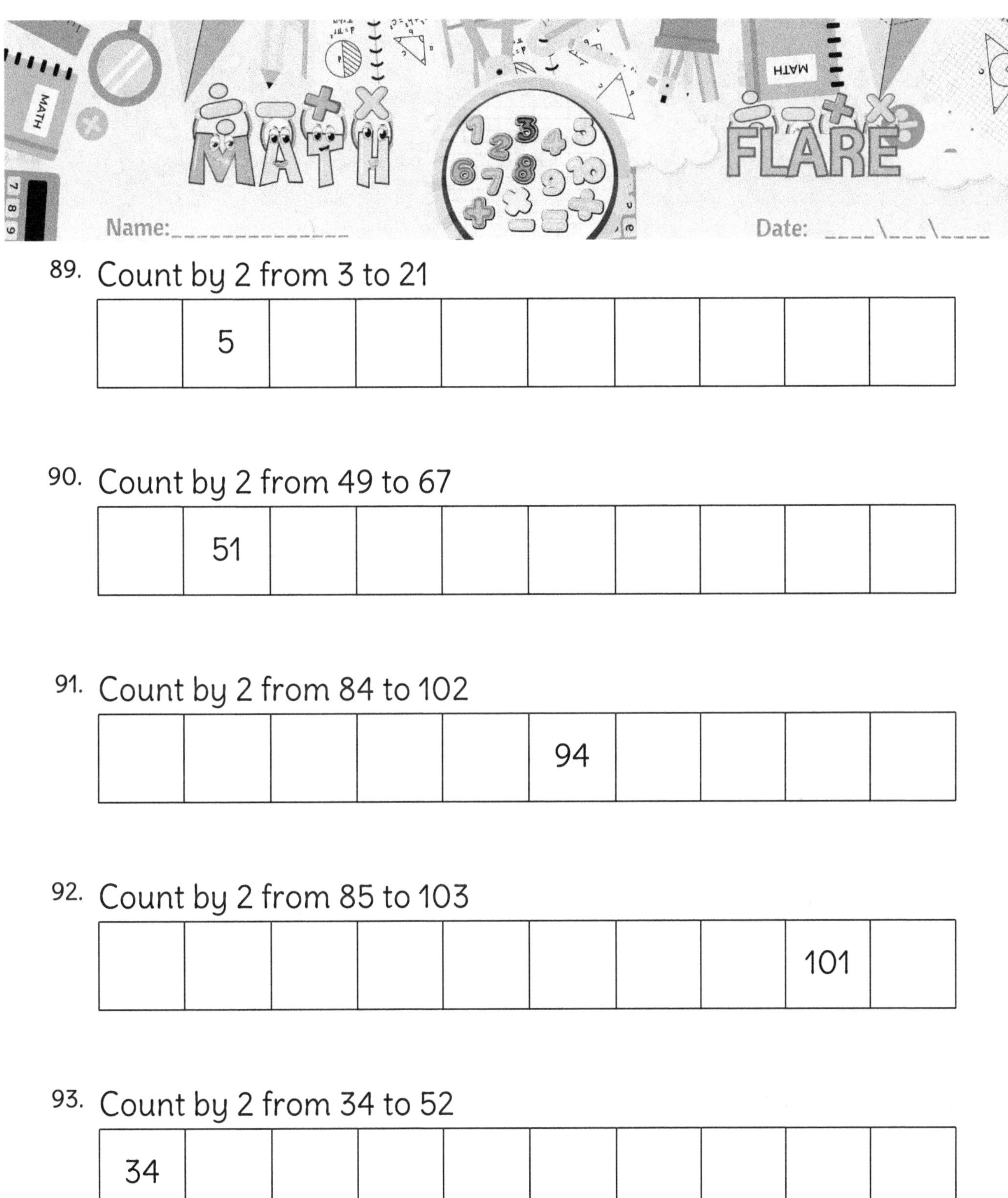

89. Count by 2 from 3 to 21

	5								

90. Count by 2 from 49 to 67

	51								

91. Count by 2 from 84 to 102

					94				

92. Count by 2 from 85 to 103

								101	

93. Count by 2 from 34 to 52

34									

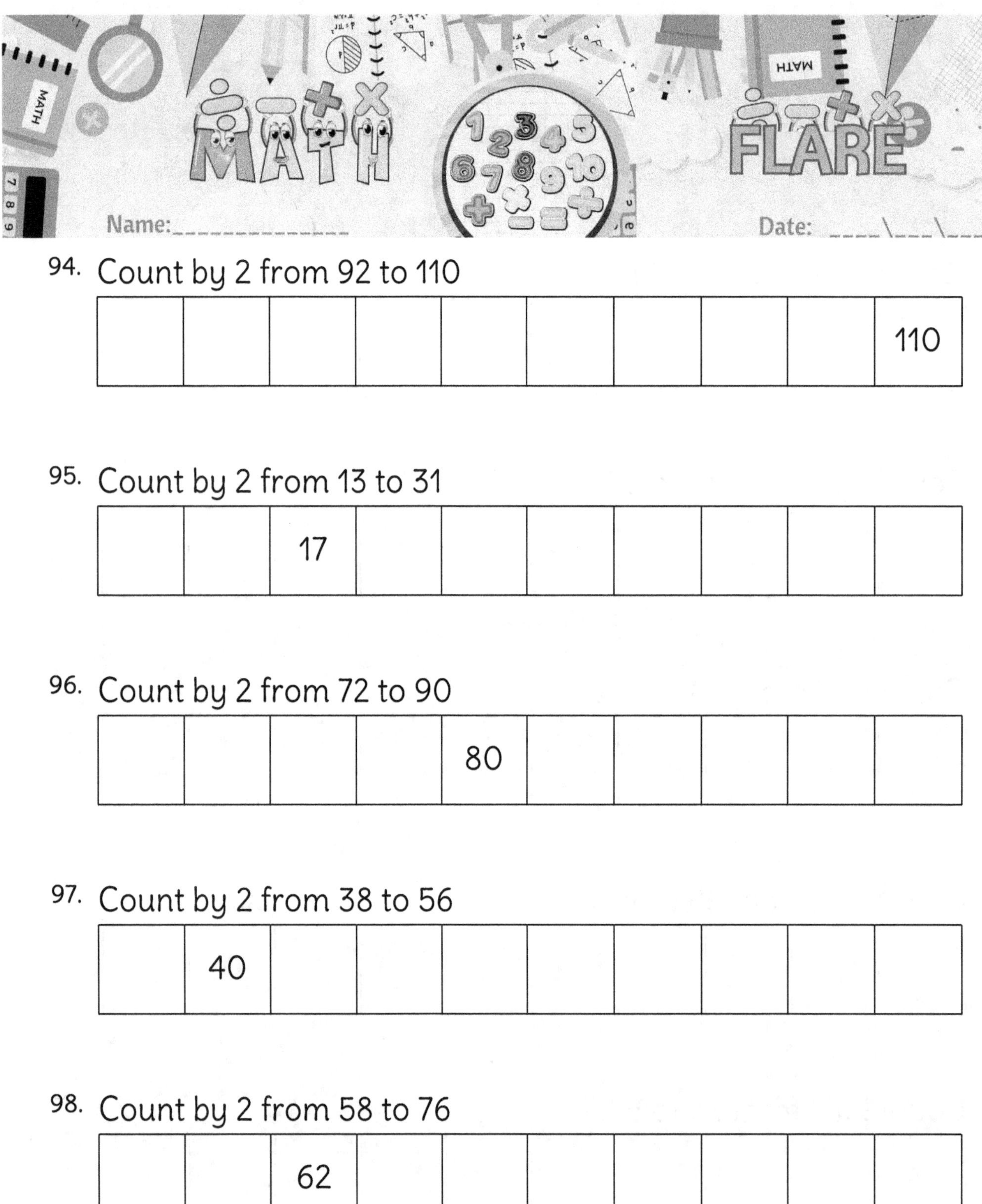

Name:_________________   Date: ____________

94. Count by 2 from 92 to 110

								110

95. Count by 2 from 13 to 31

		17						

96. Count by 2 from 72 to 90

				80				

97. Count by 2 from 38 to 56

	40							

98. Count by 2 from 58 to 76

		62						

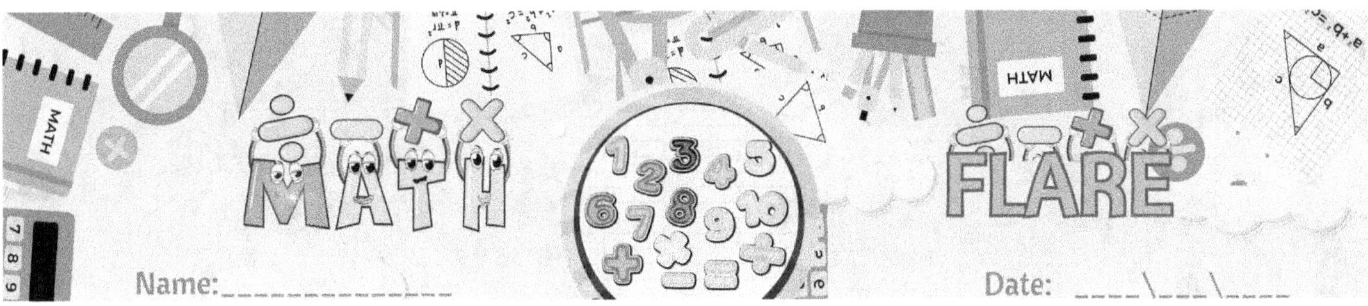

Count by 3s

Complete the counting tables.

99. Count by 3 from 11 to 38

	14							

100. Count by 3 from 33 to 60

			42					

101. Count by 3 from 89 to 116

								116

102. Count by 3 from 3 to 30

3								

103. Count by 3 from 80 to 107

			92					

104. Count by 3 from 92 to 119

	98							

105. Count by 3 from 25 to 52

28								

106. Count by 3 from 88 to 115

				103				

107. Count by 3 from 63 to 90

		72						

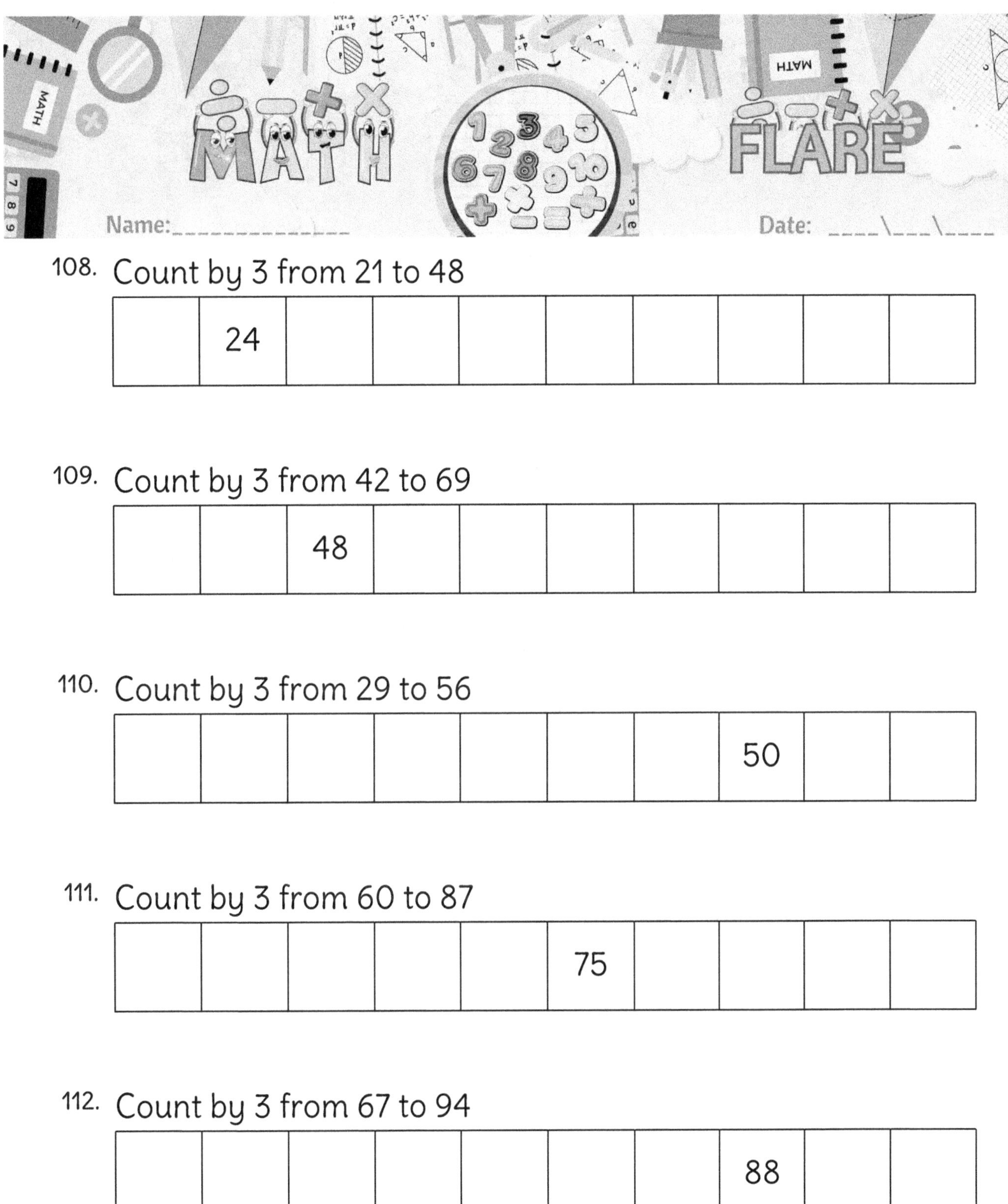

108. Count by 3 from 21 to 48

	24								

109. Count by 3 from 42 to 69

		48							

110. Count by 3 from 29 to 56

								50	

111. Count by 3 from 60 to 87

					75				

112. Count by 3 from 67 to 94

							88		

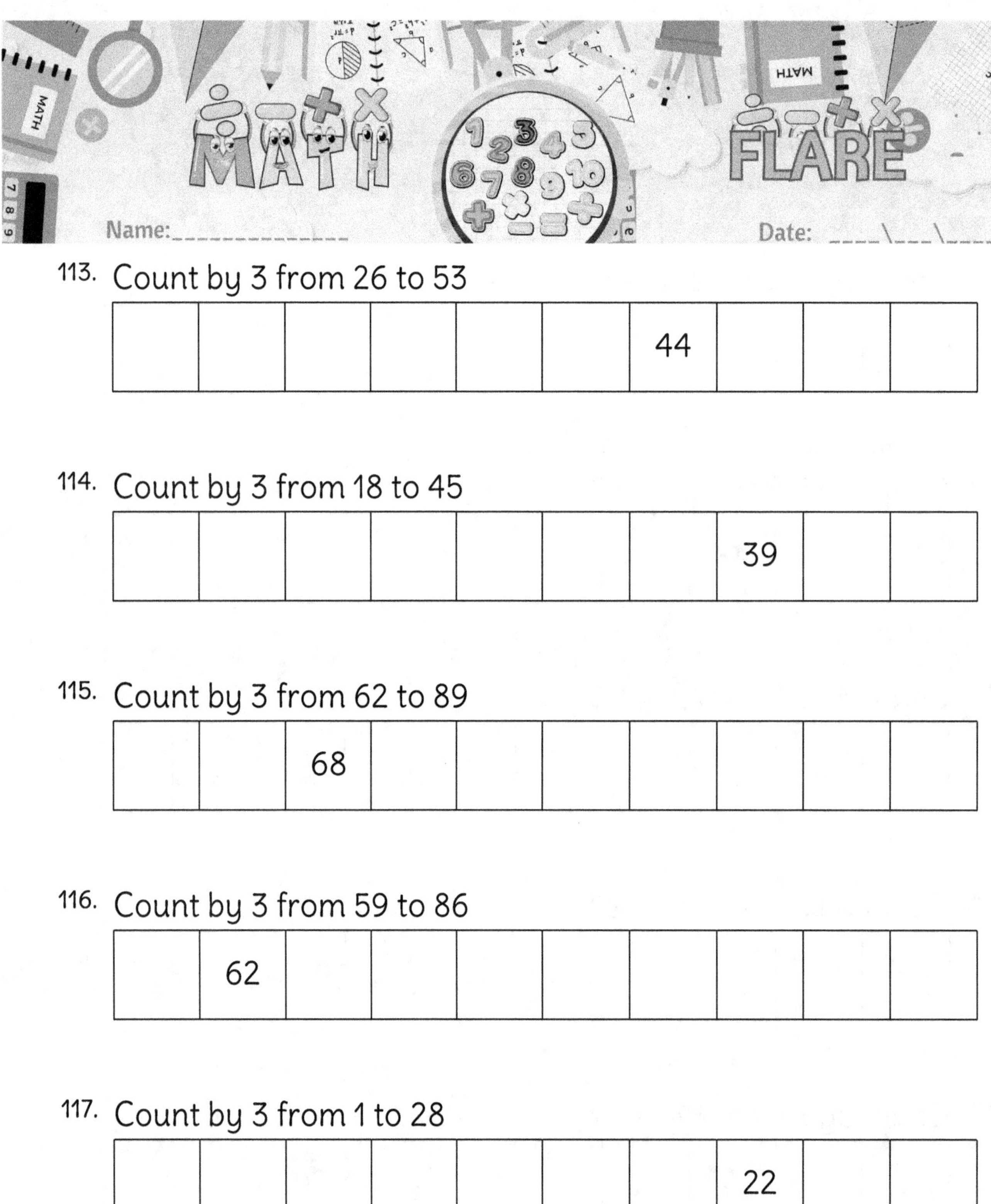

113. Count by 3 from 26 to 53

						44			

114. Count by 3 from 18 to 45

							39		

115. Count by 3 from 62 to 89

	68								

116. Count by 3 from 59 to 86

	62								

117. Count by 3 from 1 to 28

							22		

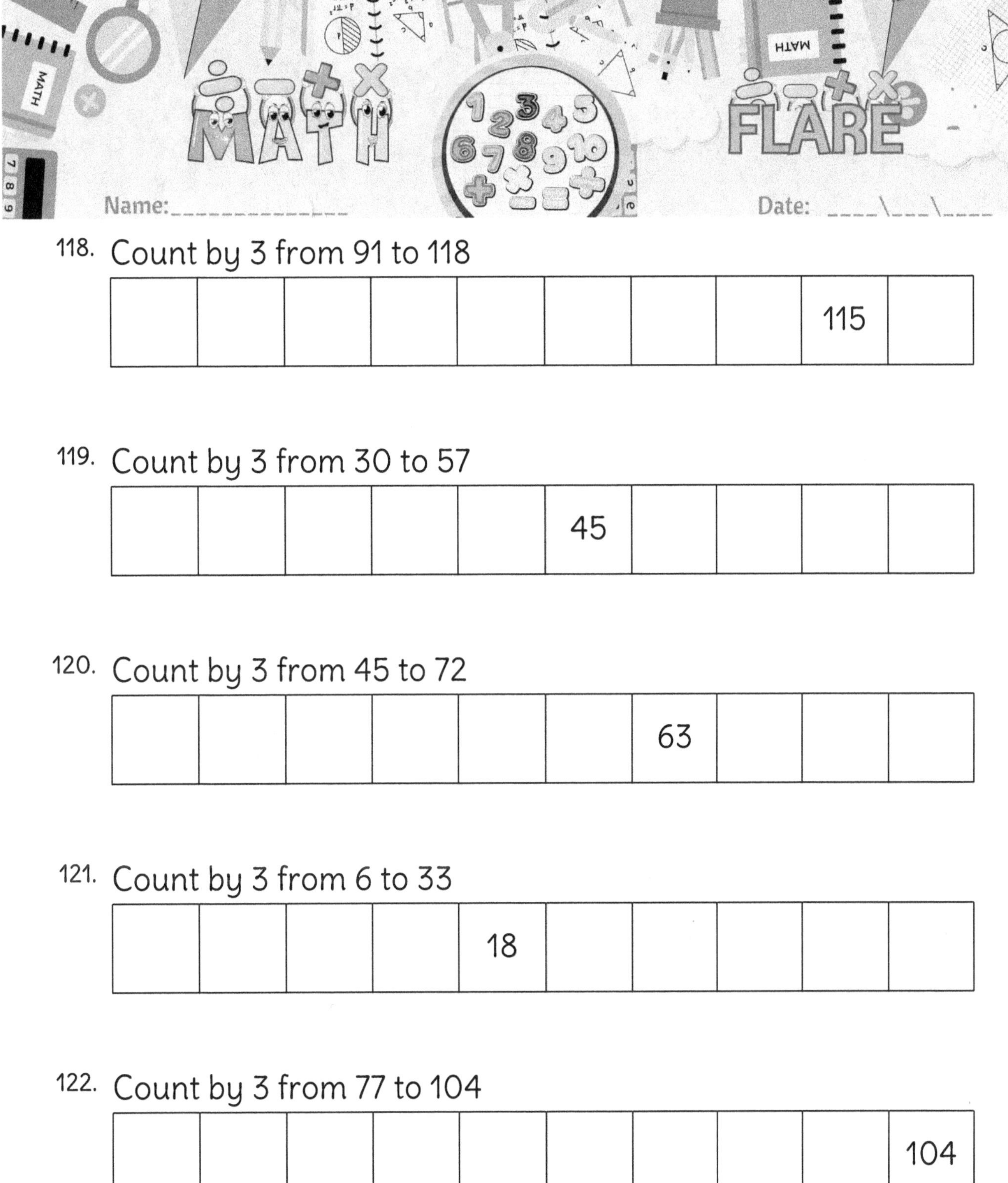

Name:________________ Date: ____________

118. Count by 3 from 91 to 118

							115	

119. Count by 3 from 30 to 57

				45				

120. Count by 3 from 45 to 72

					63			

121. Count by 3 from 6 to 33

				18				

122. Count by 3 from 77 to 104

								104

Name:______________   Date: ____________

123. Count by 3 from 51 to 78

				66				

124. Count by 3 from 8 to 35

	11							

125. Count by 3 from 57 to 84

				72				

126. Count by 3 from 34 to 61

							58	

127. Count by 3 from 17 to 44

17								

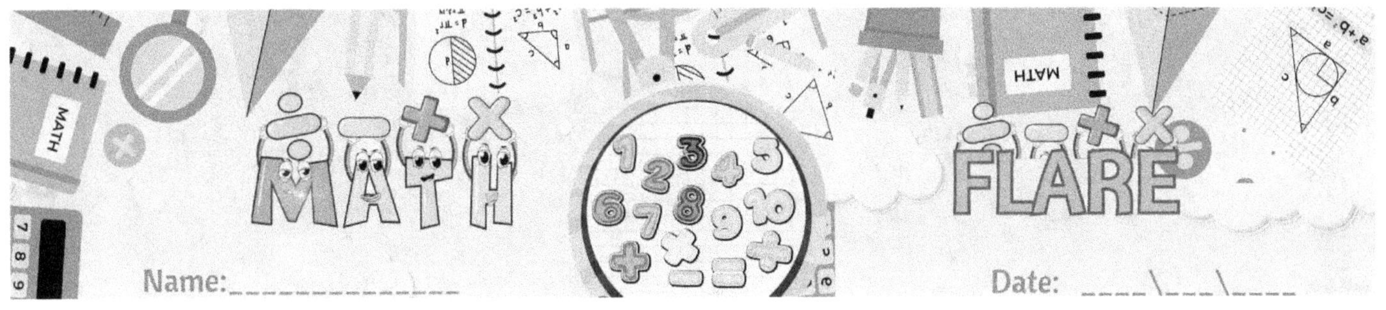

Compare the Numbers

Add: > or < or = to make the following statements true.

128. 24 ____ 57

129. 64 ____ 66

130. 91 ____ 8

131. 35 ____ 73

132. 56 ____ 32

133. 49 ____ 59

134. 45 ____ 74

135. 87 ____ 98

136. 83 ____ 58

137. 86 ____ 50

138. 9 ____ 16

139. 64 ____ 76

140. 70 ____ 96

141. 95 ____ 54

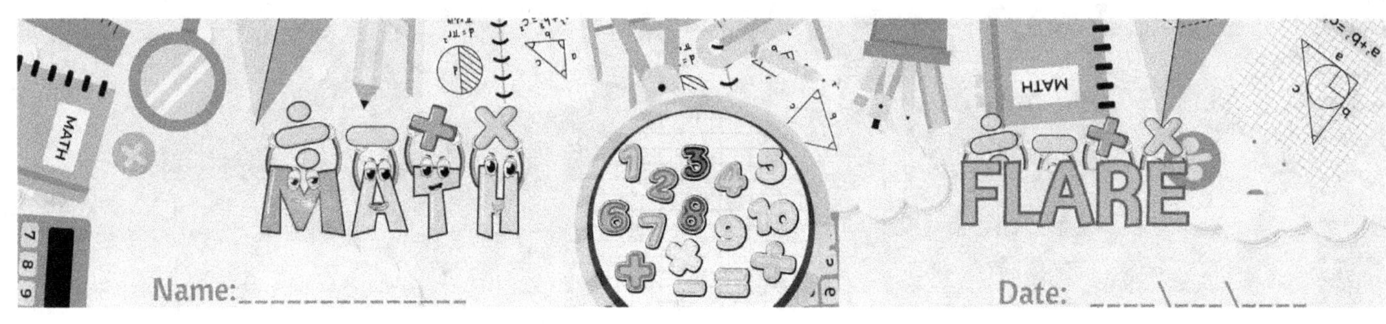

142. 52 ___ 15

143. 60 ___ 81

144. 56 ___ 21

145. 67 ___ 32

146. 60 ___ 12

147. 6 ___ 17

148. 26 ___ 57

149. 15 ___ 10

150. 96 ___ 51

151. 13 ___ 83

152. 11 ___ 71

153. 54 ___ 17

154. 69 ___ 81

155. 63 ___ 8

156. 94 ___ 88

157. 97 ___ 96

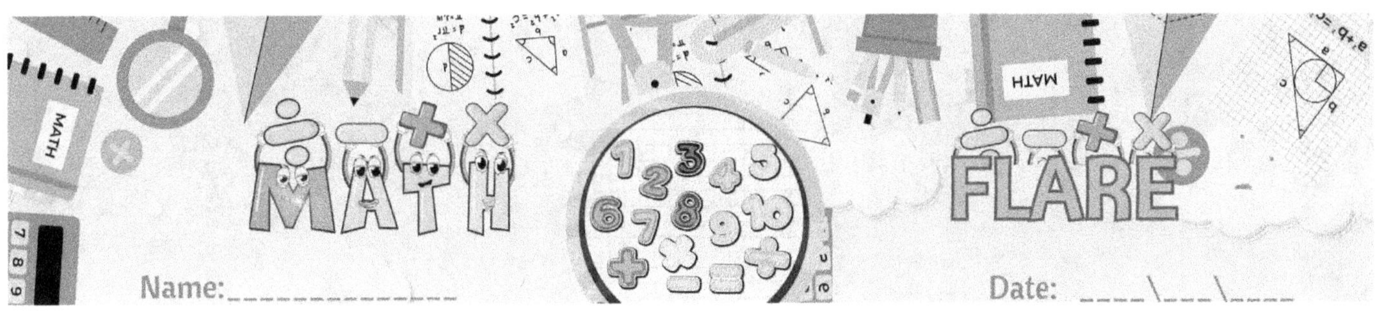

158. 13 ____ 82

159. 22 ____ 42

160. 73 ____ 69

161. 3 ____ 25

162. 7 ____ 56

163. 39 ____ 72

164. 53 ____ 69

165. 25 ____ 53

166. 2 ____ 54

167. 81 ____ 20

168. 83 ____ 13

169. 43 ____ 81

170. 61 ____ 43

171. 12 ____ 75

172. 59 ____ 60

173. 5 ____ 44

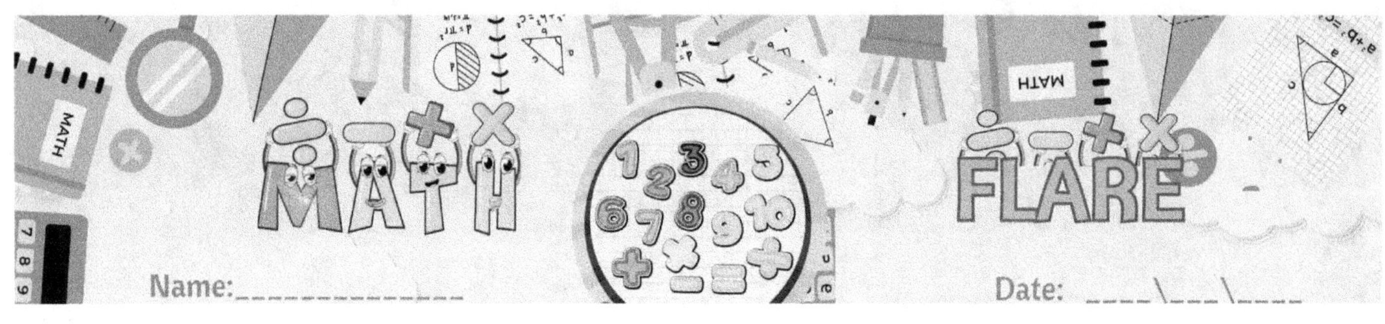

174. 38 ___ 28

175. 48 ___ 89

176. 76 ___ 56

177. 33 ___ 82

178. 64 ___ 1

179. 57 ___ 10

180. 7 ___ 40

181. 8 ___ 77

182. 13 ___ 1

183. 40 ___ 42

184. 81 ___ 30

185. 57 ___ 29

186. 66 ___ 48

187. 17 ___ 67

188. 57 ___ 43

189. 65 ___ 82

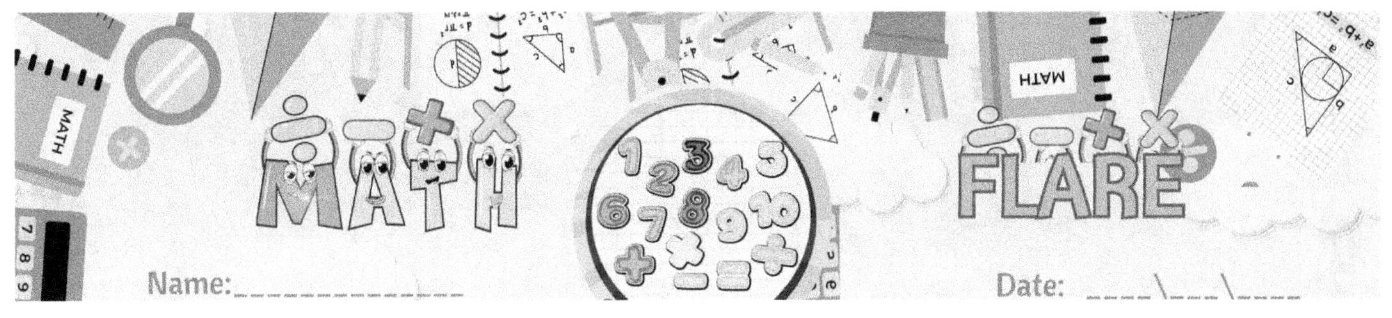

190. 18 ____ 29

191. 17 ____ 53

192. 73 ____ 94

193. 37 ____ 87

194. 48 ____ 80

195. 80 ____ 12

196. 19 ____ 49

197. 54 ____ 99

198. 64 ____ 39

199. 98 ____ 4

200. 4 ____ 93

201. 93 ____ 8

202. 71 ____ 20

203. 23 ____ 29

204. 39 ____ 67

205. 26 ____ 22

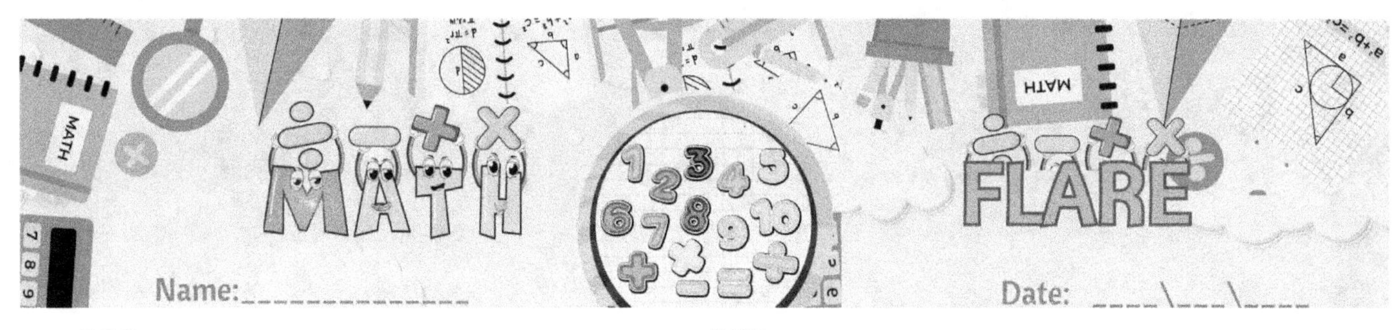

206. 36 ___ 76

207. 93 ___ 78

208. 24 ___ 55

209. 5 ___ 19

210. 65 ___ 53

211. 95 ___ 2

212. 51 ___ 46

213. 10 ___ 18

214. 94 ___ 19

215. 3 ___ 19

216. 46 ___ 61

217. 78 ___ 25

218. 37 ___ 10

219. 83 ___ 54

220. 72 ___ 8

221. 49 ___ 82

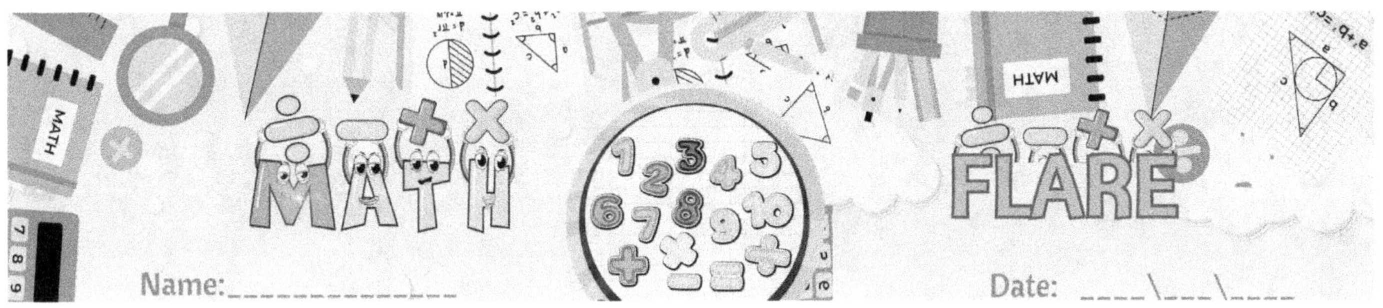

Circle the Numbers

Circle the smallest and biggest number in each group.

222.	223.	224.
80	100	25
41	22	74
3	56	47
88	51	48
1	49	40

225.	226.	227.
1	70	24
20	91	73
75	43	34
49	56	97
98	88	12

228.	229.	230.
21	94	30
73	75	27
15	17	47
92	9	77
1	62	36

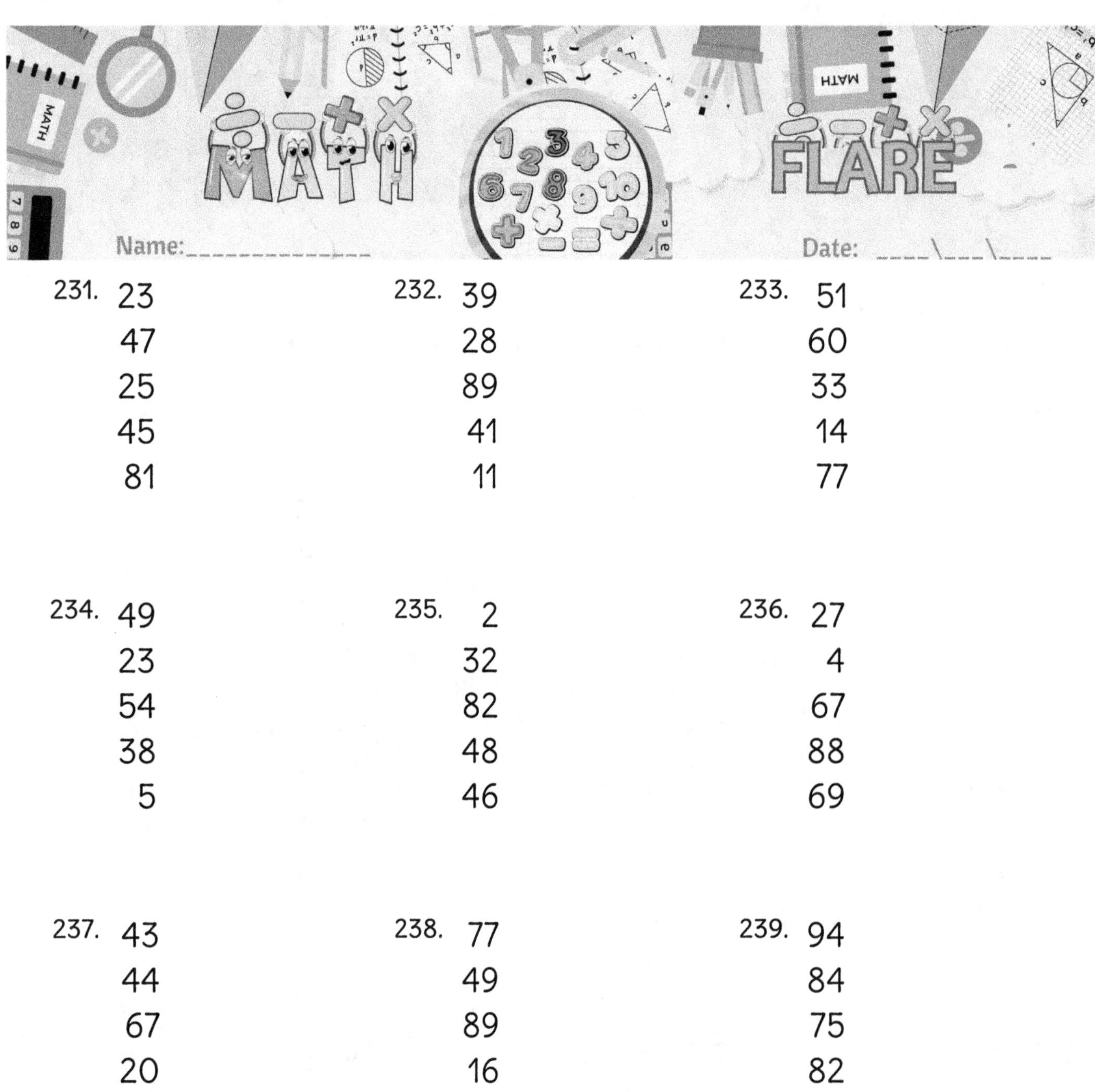

231.	232.	233.
23	39	51
47	28	60
25	89	33
45	41	14
81	11	77

234.	235.	236.
49	2	27
23	32	4
54	82	67
38	48	88
5	46	69

237.	238.	239.
43	77	94
44	49	84
67	89	75
20	16	82
65	73	51

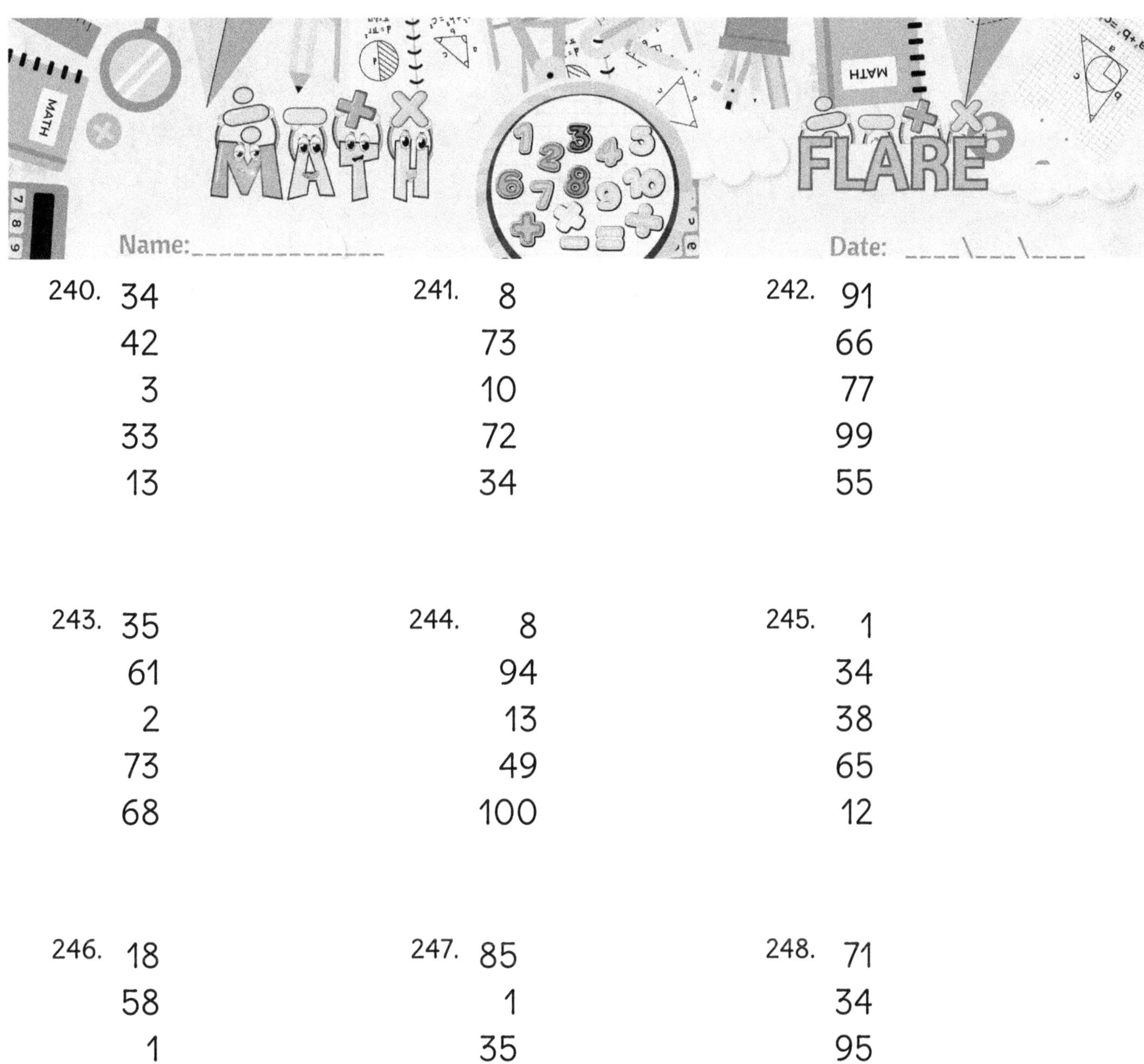

Name:________________   Date: ______________

240.	241.	242.
34	8	91
42	73	66
3	10	77
33	72	99
13	34	55

243.	244.	245.
35	8	1
61	94	34
2	13	38
73	49	65
68	100	12

246.	247.	248.
18	85	71
58	1	34
1	35	95
98	75	86
13	62	74

249.	250.	251.
12	33	40
72	83	30
91	2	55
62	14	33
38	43	12

252.	253.	254.
75	34	35
35	65	27
45	80	11
61	87	98
17	70	74

255.	256.	257.
100	43	56
28	77	87
75	27	55
89	79	73
30	36	47

258.
2
64
88
36
89

259.
34
70
41
47
92

260.
4
92
6
56
16

261.
69
41
3
81
45

262.
83
32
59
18
81

263.
78
26
14
15
89

264.
26
64
24
63
85

265.
66
58
34
42
38

266.
40
85
23
73
80

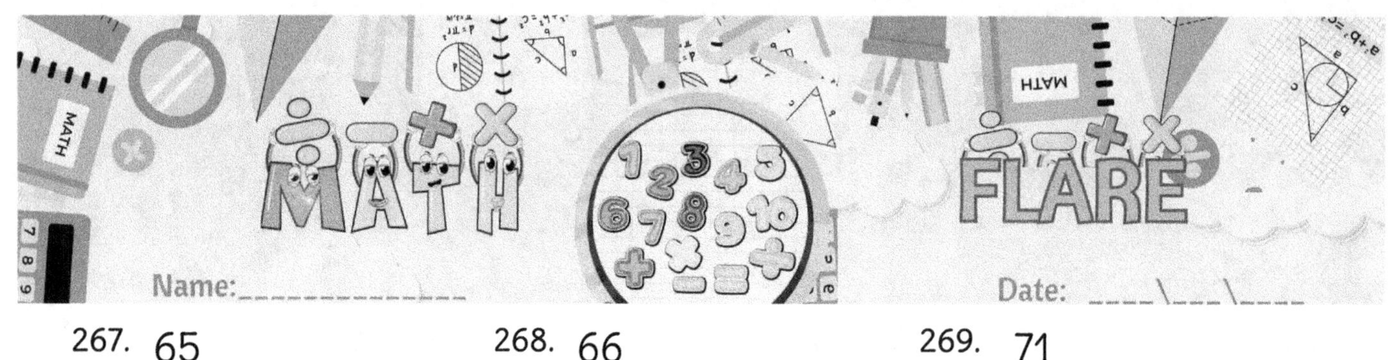

267.	65	268.	66	269.	71
	72		58		52
	86		81		89
	33		57		63
	54		77		70

270.	67	271.	93	272.	45
	91		69		47
	78		54		3
	16		84		46
	81		76		93

273.	75	274.	7	275.	68
	95		40		84
	10		81		67
	2		62		87
	14		23		15

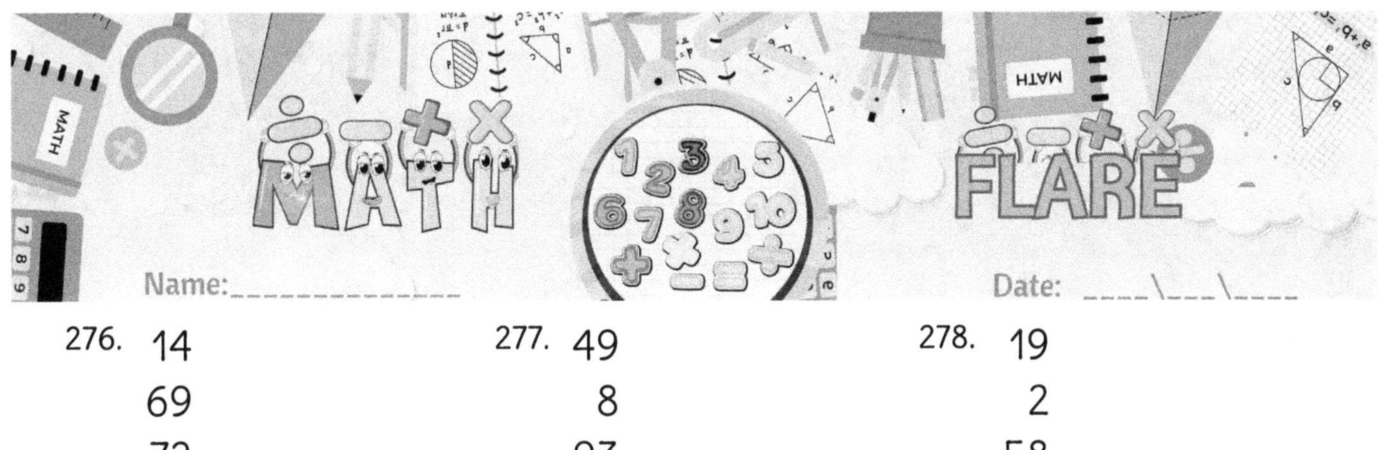

276. 14
      69
      72
      73
      71

277. 49
      8
      93
      88
      97

278. 19
      2
      58
      9
      20

279. 55
      36
      65
      3
      76

280. 43
      88
      50
      63
      28

281. 10
      17
      94
      13
      2

282. 68
      70
      62
      76
      31

283. 75
      44
      67
      88
      17

284. 15
      18
      89
      38
      24

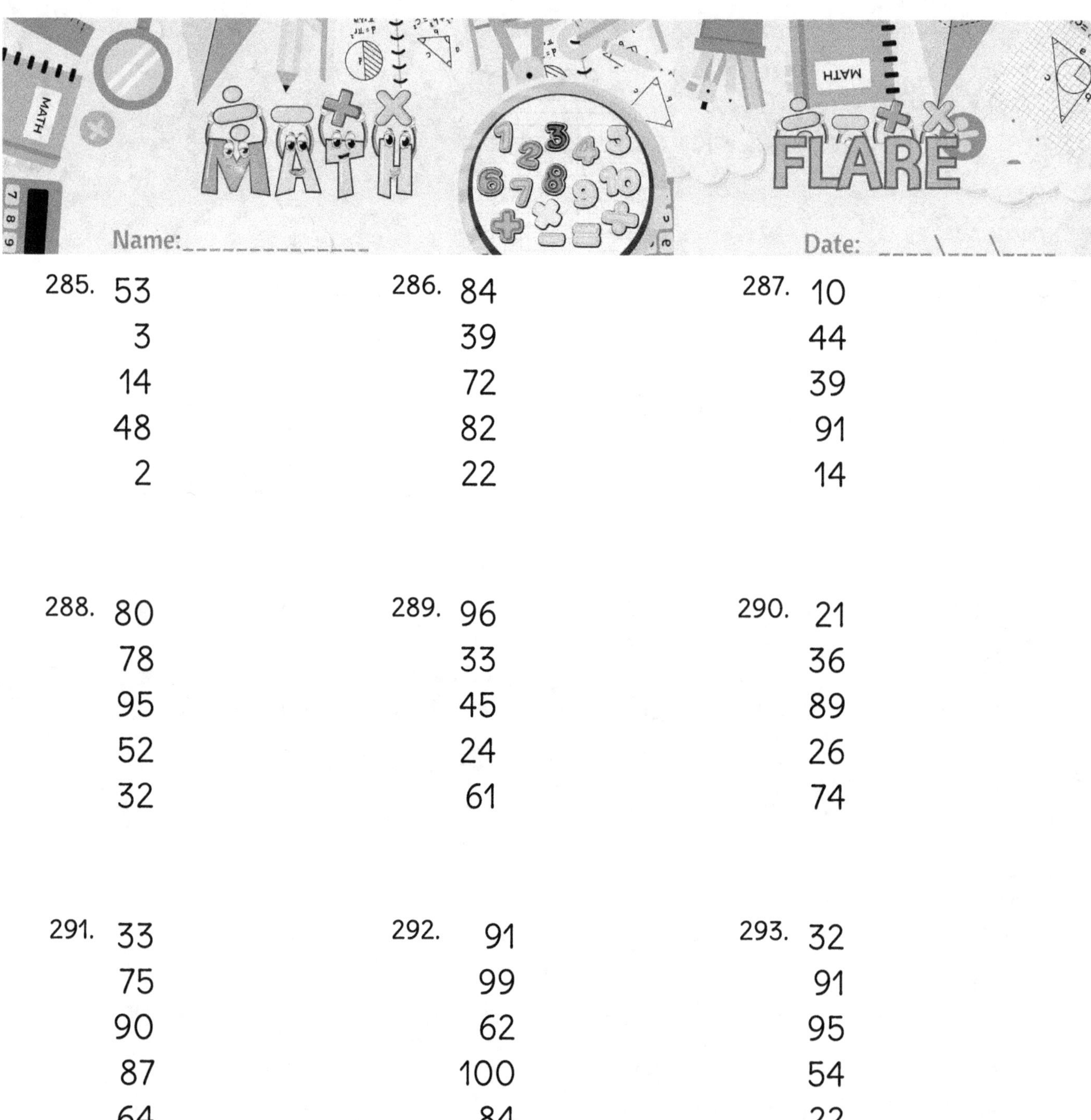

285. 53
3
14
48
2

286. 84
39
72
82
22

287. 10
44
39
91
14

288. 80
78
95
52
32

289. 96
33
45
24
61

290. 21
36
89
26
74

291. 33
75
90
87
64

292. 91
99
62
100
84

293. 32
91
95
54
22

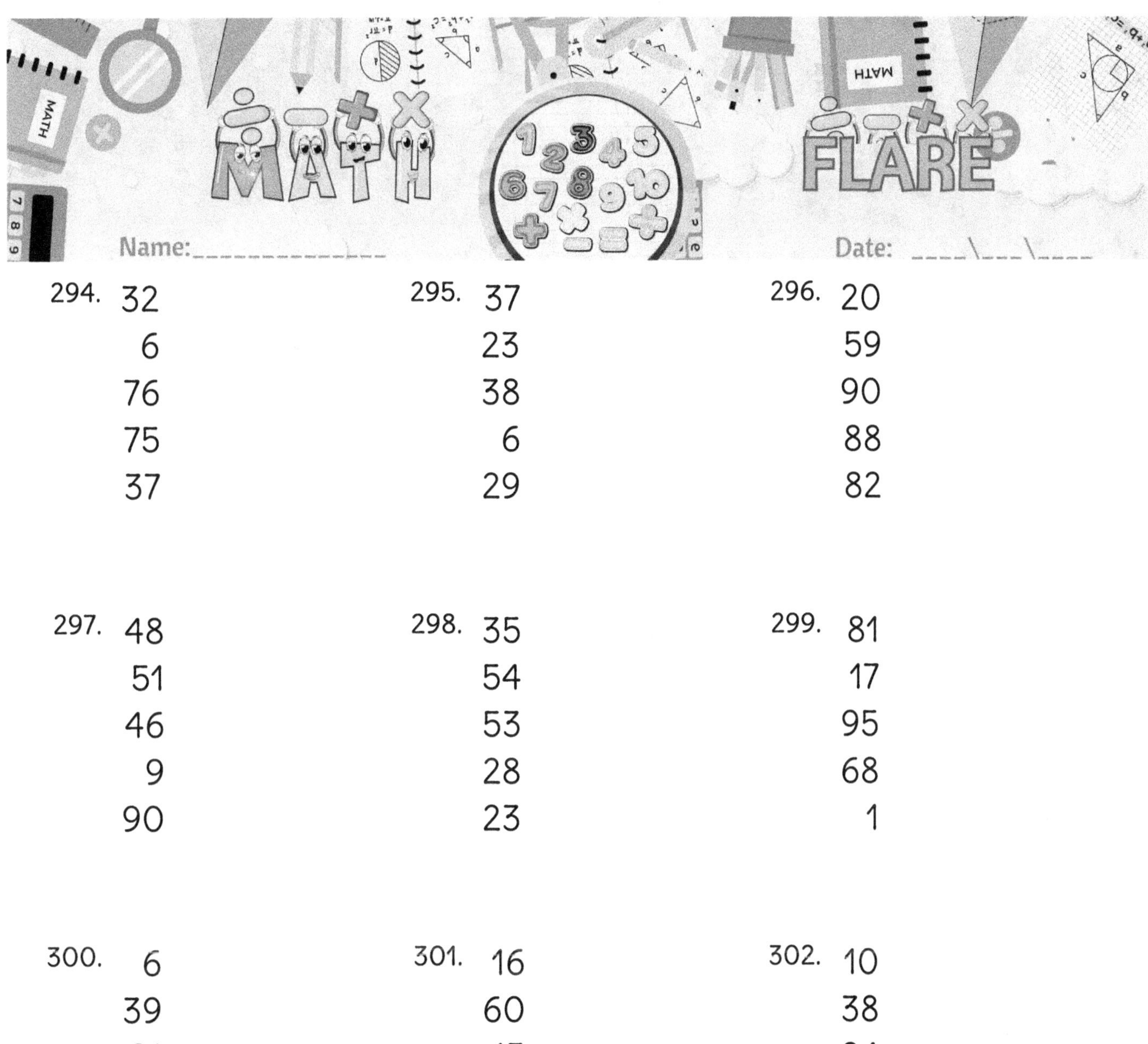

294.	295.	296.
32	37	20
6	23	59
76	38	90
75	6	88
37	29	82

297.	298.	299.
48	35	81
51	54	17
46	53	95
9	28	68
90	23	1

300.	301.	302.
6	16	10
39	60	38
91	15	84
3	89	58
29	37	45

303.	304.	305.
33	82	53
10	45	49
74	87	52
19	65	56
36	79	21

306.	307.	308.
29	68	37
70	88	58
6	60	72
23	66	80
81	89	98

309.	310.	311.
71	43	53
95	76	26
83	32	16
91	19	51
72	61	64

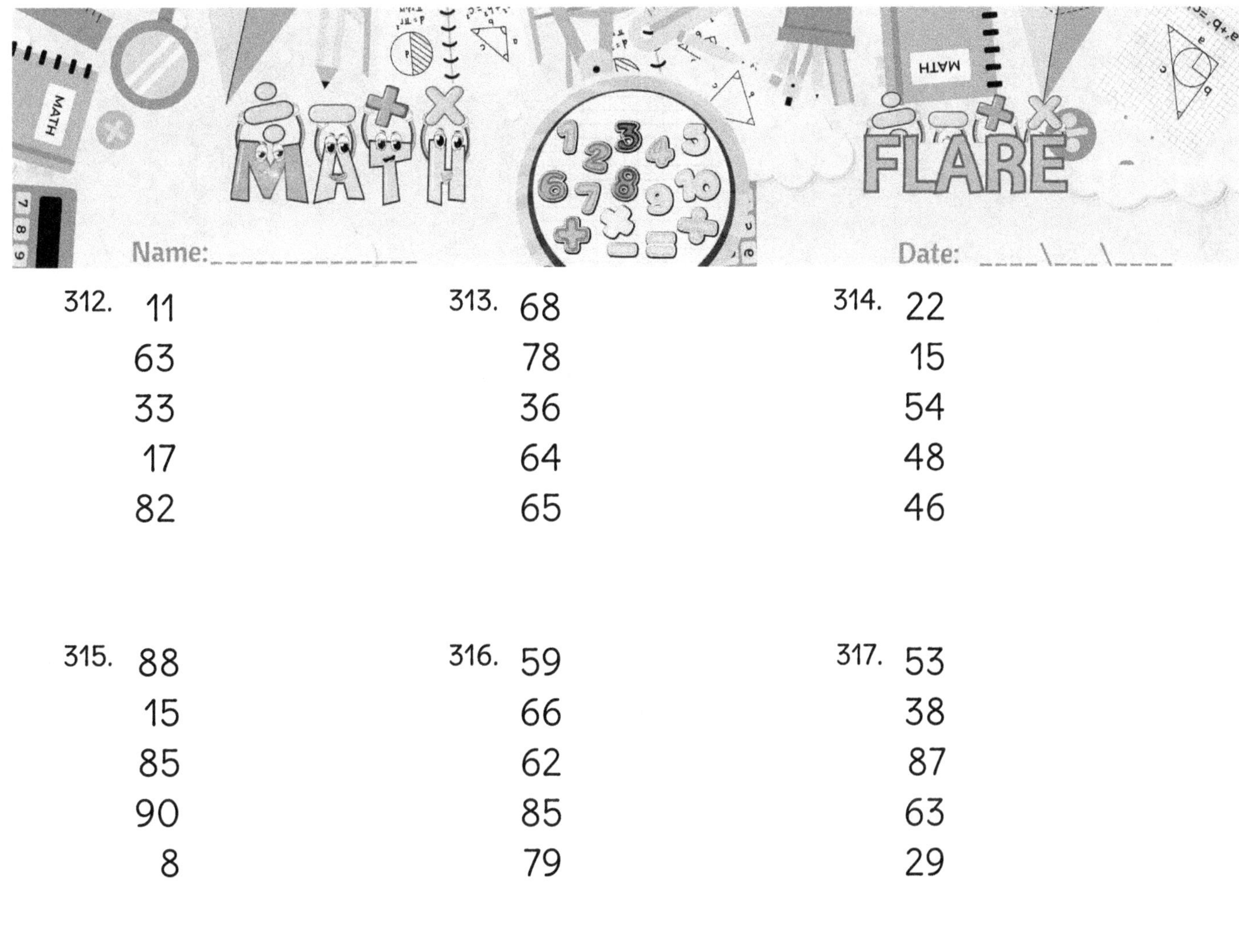

312.	313.	314.
11	68	22
63	78	15
33	36	54
17	64	48
82	65	46

315.	316.	317.
88	59	53
15	66	38
85	62	87
90	85	63
8	79	29

318.	319.	320.
42	74	93
72	25	60
9	56	20
3	99	26
78	30	50

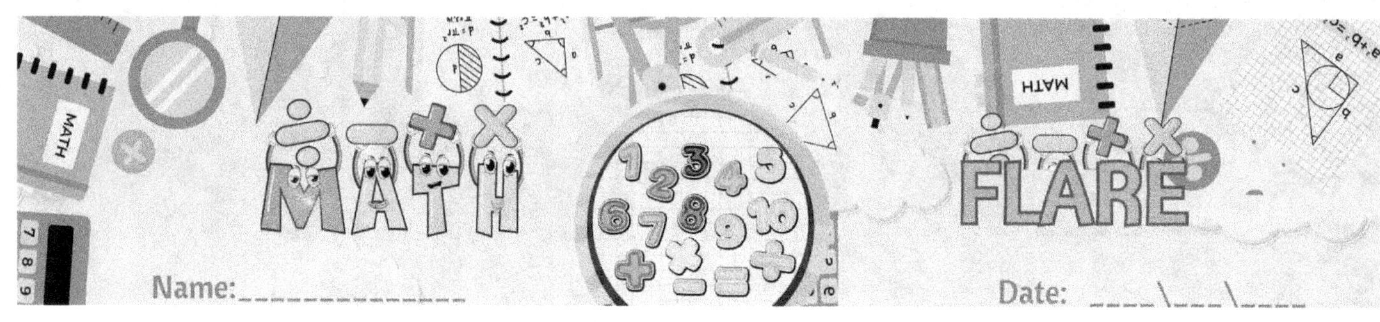

Missing Numbers

Fill in the missing numbers, before and after and between.

321. 28 _____

322. _____ 86 _____

323. _____ 75

324. _____ 42

325. 43 _____

326. 45 _____

327. _____ 50

328. _____ 30

329. _____ 93 _____

330. 35 _____

331. 51 _____

332. _____ 52 _____

333. _____ 73 _____

334. 59 _____ 61

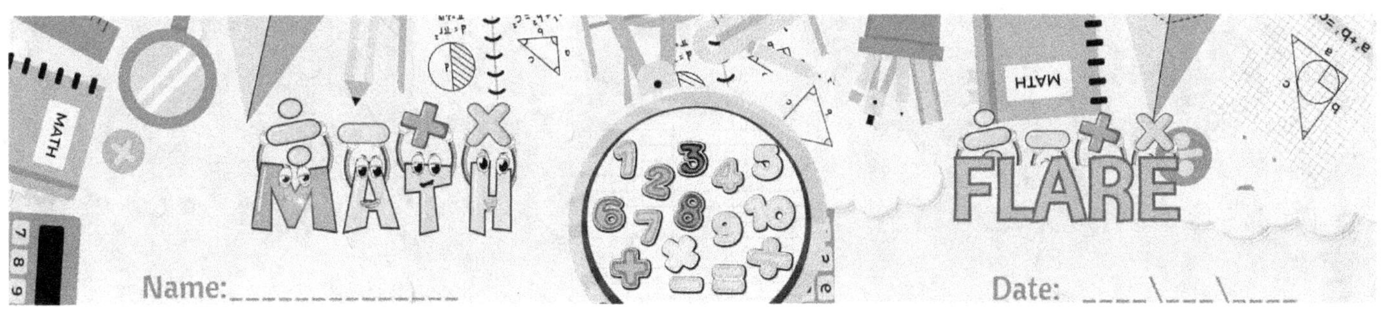

335. 60 ____

336. ____ 100

337. ____ 37

338. ____ 52

339. 53 ____

340. 90 ____ 92

341. ___ 3

342. 67 ____ 69

343. ____ 34 ____

344. 76 ____

345. 71 ____ 73

346. 2 ___ 4

347. 85 ____

348. 100 ____

349. 73 ____

350. 2 ___

351. _____ 81 _____

352. _____ 68

353. 7 ___ 9

354. 67 _____

355. 88 _____ 90

356. 77 _____ 79

357. _____ 85

358. 22 _____

359. _____ 41 _____

360. 38 _____

361. _____ 89

362. ____ 18 ____

363. 15 _____

364. _____ 64

365. _____ 59

366. 12 _____ 14

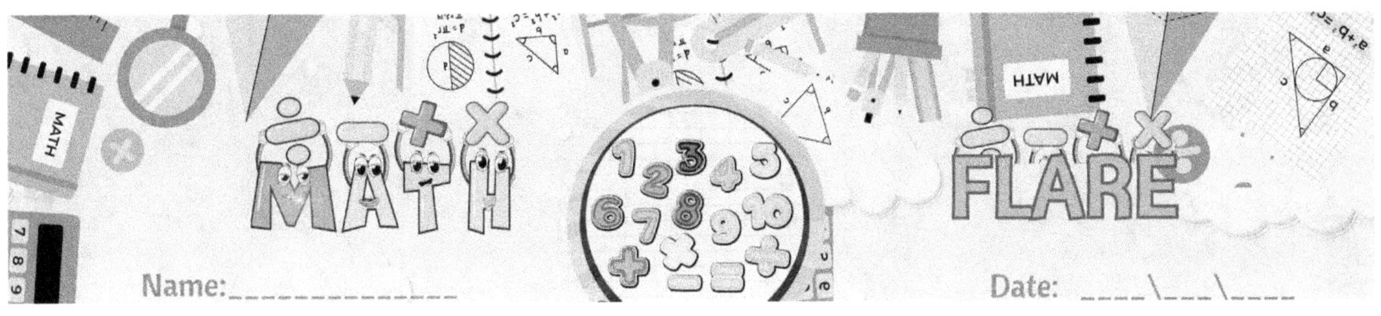

367. ____ 12

368. ______ 81

369. ____ 92

370. ___ 7 ___

371. ____ 32 _____

372. 23 _____

373. ___ 5

374. 81 _____ 83

375. 83 _____

376. 78 _____

377. _____ 24

378. 39 _____

379. 13 ____ 15

380. _____ 38

381. _____ 43

382. 68 _____

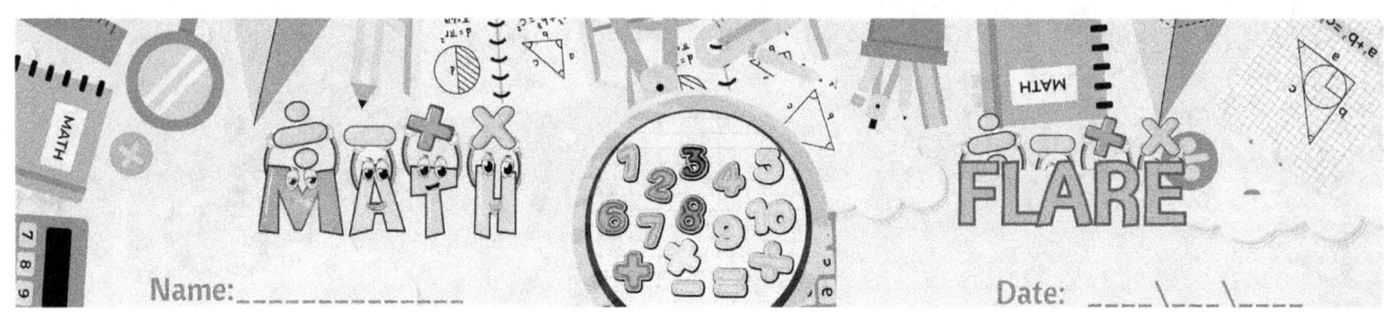

383. 34 _____ 36

384. 26 _____ 28

385. 63 _____

386. _____ 97

387. _____ 11

388. 38 _____ 40

389. 9 _____

390. _____ 55

391. _____ 47

392. 61 _____

393. _____ 58 _____

394. ___ 9 _____

395. 29 _____ 31

396. _____ 100 _____

397. _____ 84 _____

398. 30 _____ 32

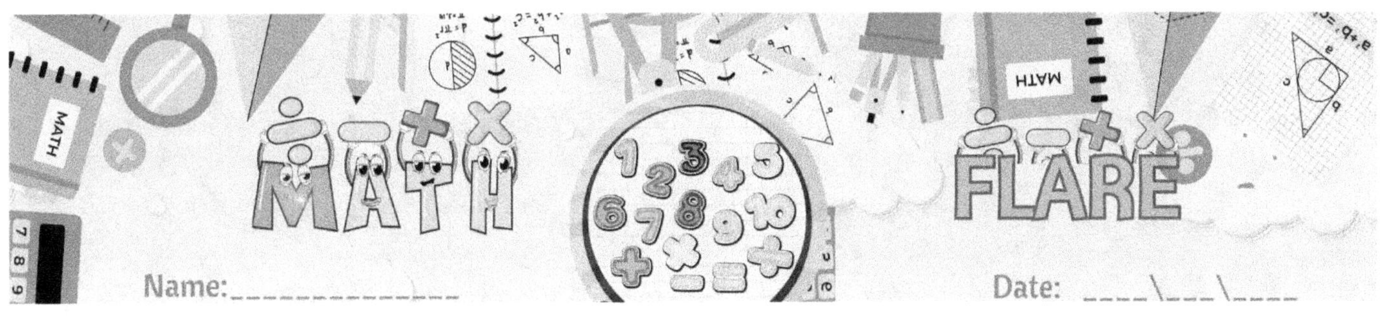

399. 56 _____ 58

400. 7 ___

401. 69 _____ 71

402. 6 ___ 8

403. 69 _____

404. 87 _____

405. 13 _____

406. _____ 80 _____

407. _____ 49 _____

408. _____ 69 _____

409. _____ 72 _____

410. 5 ___

411. _____ 45

412. _____ 17 _____

413. 36 _____

414. _____ 17

ANSWERS

Page 1:   Skip Counting: Ascending

1.

Count by 1 from 1 to 100

1	2	3	4	5	6	7	8	9	10
11	12	13	14	15	16	17	18	19	20
21	22	23	24	25	26	27	28	29	30
31	32	33	34	35	36	37	38	39	40
41	42	43	44	45	46	47	48	49	50
51	52	53	54	55	56	57	58	59	60
61	62	63	64	65	66	67	68	69	70
71	72	73	74	75	76	77	78	79	80
81	82	83	84	85	86	87	88	89	90
91	92	93	94	95	96	97	98	99	100

Page 2:   Skip Counting: Ascending

2.

Count by 1 from 1 to 100

1	2	3	4	5	6	7	8	9	10
11	12	13	14	15	16	17	18	19	20
21	22	23	24	25	26	27	28	29	30
31	32	33	34	35	36	37	38	39	40
41	42	43	44	45	46	47	48	49	50
51	52	53	54	55	56	57	58	59	60
61	62	63	64	65	66	67	68	69	70
71	72	73	74	75	76	77	78	79	80
81	82	83	84	85	86	87	88	89	90
91	92	93	94	95	96	97	98	99	100

Page 3:   Skip Counting: Ascending

3.

Count by 1 from 1 to 100

1	2	3	4	5	6	7	8	9	10
11	12	13	14	15	16	17	18	19	20
21	22	23	24	25	26	27	28	29	30
31	32	33	34	35	36	37	38	39	40
41	42	43	44	45	46	47	48	49	50
51	52	53	54	55	56	57	58	59	60
61	62	63	64	65	66	67	68	69	70
71	72	73	74	75	76	77	78	79	80
81	82	83	84	85	86	87	88	89	90
91	92	93	94	95	96	97	98	99	100

Page 4:   Count Up

4.

62	63	64	65	66	67	68	69	70	71

5.

| 53 | 54 | 55 | 56 | **57** | **58** | 59 | 60 | 61 | 62 |

6.

| **77** | **78** | 79 | 80 | 81 | 82 | 83 | 84 | 85 | 86 |

7.

| 22 | 23 | 24 | 25 | 26 | 27 | **28** | **29** | 30 | 31 |

8.

| 39 | **40** | **41** | 42 | 43 | 44 | 45 | 46 | 47 | 48 |

9.

| 60 | 61 | **62** | **63** | 64 | 65 | 66 | 67 | 68 | 69 |

10.

| 29 | 30 | 31 | 32 | **33** | **34** | 35 | 36 | 37 | 38 |

11.

| 68 | 69 | 70 | 71 | 72 | 73 | 74 | 75 | 76 | 77 |

12.

| 98 | **99** | **100** | 101 | 102 | 103 | 104 | 105 | 106 | 107 |

13.

| **91** | **92** | 93 | 94 | 95 | 96 | 97 | 98 | 99 | 100 |

14.

| 4 | 5 | 6 | 7 | **8** | **9** | 10 | 11 | 12 | 13 |

15.

| 58 | 59 | 60 | **61** | **62** | 63 | 64 | 65 | 66 | 67 |

16.

| 72 | 73 | 74 | 75 | 76 | 77 | **78** | **79** | 80 | 81 |

17.

| 44 | 45 | 46 | 47 | **48** | **49** | 50 | 51 | 52 | 53 |

18.

| 100 | **101** | **102** | 103 | 104 | 105 | 106 | 107 | 108 | 109 |

19.

| 37 | 38 | 39 | 40 | **41** | **42** | 43 | 44 | 45 | 46 |

20.

| 28 | **29** | **30** | 31 | 32 | 33 | 34 | 35 | 36 | 37 |

21.

| **35** | **36** | 37 | 38 | 39 | 40 | 41 | 42 | 43 | 44 |

22.

| **71** | **72** | 73 | 74 | 75 | 76 | 77 | 78 | 79 | 80 |

23.

| **81** | **82** | 83 | 84 | 85 | 86 | 87 | 88 | 89 | 90 |

24.

| 9 | 10 | 11 | 12 | 13 | 14 | 15 | **16** | **17** | 18 |

25.

| 30 | 31 | **32** | **33** | 34 | 35 | 36 | 37 | 38 | 39 |

26.

| 19 | **20** | **21** | 22 | 23 | 24 | 25 | 26 | 27 | 28 |

27.

| 51 | 52 | 53 | 54 | 55 | 56 | 57 | 58 | 59 | 60 |

28.

| 26 | 27 | 28 | 29 | 30 | 31 | 32 | 33 | 34 | 35 |

29.

| 50 | 51 | 52 | 53 | 54 | 55 | 56 | 57 | 58 | 59 |

30.

| 11 | 12 | 13 | 14 | 15 | 16 | 17 | 18 | 19 | 20 |

31.

| 17 | 18 | 19 | 20 | 21 | 22 | 23 | 24 | 25 | 26 |

32.

| 96 | 97 | 98 | 99 | 100 | 101 | 102 | 103 | 104 | 105 |

33.

| 8 | 9 | 10 | 11 | 12 | 13 | 14 | 15 | 16 | 17 |

34.

| 14 | 15 | 16 | 17 | 18 | 19 | 20 | 21 | 22 | 23 |

35.

| 69 | 70 | 71 | 72 | 73 | 74 | 75 | 76 | 77 | 78 |

36.

| 25 | 26 | 27 | 28 | 29 | 30 | 31 | 32 | 33 | 34 |

Page 9: Count Down

37.

| 80 | 79 | 78 | 77 | 76 | 75 | 74 | 73 | 72 | 71 |

38. | 18 | 17 | 16 | 15 | 14 | 13 | 12 | 11 | 10 | 9 |

39. | 69 | 68 | 67 | 66 | 65 | 64 | 63 | 62 | 61 | 60 |

40. | 39 | 38 | 37 | 36 | 35 | 34 | 33 | 32 | 31 | 30 |

41. | 41 | 40 | 39 | 38 | 37 | 36 | 35 | 34 | 33 | 32 |

42. | 13 | 12 | 11 | 10 | 9 | 8 | 7 | 6 | 5 | 4 |

43. | 44 | 43 | 42 | 41 | 40 | 39 | 38 | 37 | 36 | 35 |

44. | 67 | 66 | 65 | 64 | 63 | 62 | 61 | 60 | 59 | 58 |

45. | 38 | 37 | 36 | 35 | 34 | 33 | 32 | 31 | 30 | 29 |

46. | 43 | 42 | 41 | 40 | 39 | 38 | 37 | 36 | 35 | 34 |

47. | 23 | 22 | 21 | 20 | 19 | 18 | 17 | 16 | 15 | 14 |

48. | 57 | 56 | 55 | 54 | 53 | 52 | 51 | 50 | 49 | 48 |

49. | 10 | 9 | 8 | 7 | 6 | 5 | 4 | 3 | 2 | 1 |

50. | 78 | 77 | 76 | 75 | 74 | 73 | 72 | 71 | 70 | 69 |

51. | 51 | 50 | 49 | 48 | 47 | 46 | 45 | 44 | 43 | 42 |

52. | 64 | 63 | 62 | 61 | 60 | 59 | 58 | 57 | 56 | 55 |

53. | 30 | 29 | 28 | 27 | 26 | 25 | 24 | 23 | 22 | 21 |

54. | 17 | 16 | 15 | 14 | 13 | 12 | 11 | 10 | 9 | 8 |

55. | 89 | 88 | 87 | 86 | 85 | 84 | 83 | 82 | 81 | 80 |

56. | 81 | 80 | 79 | 78 | 77 | 76 | 75 | 74 | 73 | 72 |

57. | 61 | 60 | 59 | 58 | 57 | 56 | 55 | 54 | 53 | 52 |

58. | 83 | 82 | 81 | 80 | 79 | 78 | 77 | 76 | 75 | 74 |

59. | 96 | 95 | 94 | 93 | 92 | 91 | 90 | 89 | 88 | 87 |

60.

| 49 | 48 | 47 | 46 | 45 | 44 | 43 | 42 | 41 | 40 |

61.

| 54 | 53 | 52 | 51 | 50 | 49 | 48 | 47 | 46 | 45 |

62.

| 62 | 61 | 60 | 59 | 58 | 57 | 56 | 55 | 54 | 53 |

63.

| 77 | 76 | 75 | 74 | 73 | 72 | 71 | 70 | 69 | 68 |

64.

| 53 | 52 | 51 | 50 | 49 | 48 | 47 | 46 | 45 | 44 |

65.

| 20 | 19 | 18 | 17 | 16 | 15 | 14 | 13 | 12 | 11 |

66.

| 32 | 31 | 30 | 29 | 28 | 27 | 26 | 25 | 24 | 23 |

67.

| 14 | 13 | 12 | 11 | 10 | 9 | 8 | 7 | 6 | 5 |

68.

| 11 | 10 | 9 | 8 | 7 | 6 | 5 | 4 | 3 | 2 |

69.

| 50 | 49 | 48 | 47 | 46 | 45 | 44 | 43 | 42 | 41 |

Page 14: Count by 2s

70.

| 91 | 93 | 95 | 97 | 99 | 101 | 103 | 105 | 107 | 109 |

71.	87	89	91	93	95	97	99	101	103	105
72.	11	13	15	17	19	21	23	25	27	29
73.	43	45	47	49	51	53	55	57	59	61
74.	70	72	74	76	78	80	82	84	86	88
75.	16	18	20	22	24	26	28	30	32	34
76.	23	25	27	29	31	33	35	37	39	41
77.	54	56	58	60	62	64	66	68	70	72
78.	22	24	26	28	30	32	34	36	38	40
79.	20	22	24	26	28	30	32	34	36	38
80.	80	82	84	86	88	90	92	94	96	98
81.	5	7	9	11	13	15	17	19	21	23

82.

| 27 | 29 | 31 | 33 | 35 | **37** | 39 | 41 | 43 | 45 |

83.

| 42 | 44 | 46 | 48 | 50 | 52 | **54** | 56 | 58 | 60 |

84.

| 32 | 34 | 36 | 38 | 40 | 42 | 44 | 46 | **48** | 50 |

85.

| 18 | 20 | 22 | 24 | 26 | 28 | 30 | 32 | 34 | **36** |

86.

| **47** | 49 | 51 | 53 | 55 | 57 | 59 | 61 | 63 | 65 |

87.

| 60 | 62 | **64** | 66 | 68 | 70 | 72 | 74 | 76 | 78 |

88.

| 96 | 98 | 100 | 102 | 104 | **106** | 108 | 110 | 112 | 114 |

89.

| 3 | **5** | 7 | 9 | 11 | 13 | 15 | 17 | 19 | 21 |

90.

| 49 | **51** | 53 | 55 | 57 | 59 | 61 | 63 | 65 | 67 |

91.

| 84 | 86 | 88 | 90 | 92 | **94** | 96 | 98 | 100 | 102 |

92.

| 85 | 87 | 89 | 91 | 93 | 95 | 97 | 99 | **101** | 103 |

93.

| 34 | 36 | 38 | 40 | 42 | 44 | 46 | 48 | 50 | 52 |

94.

| 92 | 94 | 96 | 98 | 100 | 102 | 104 | 106 | 108 | 110 |

95.

| 13 | 15 | 17 | 19 | 21 | 23 | 25 | 27 | 29 | 31 |

96.

| 72 | 74 | 76 | 78 | 80 | 82 | 84 | 86 | 88 | 90 |

97.

| 38 | 40 | 42 | 44 | 46 | 48 | 50 | 52 | 54 | 56 |

98.

| 58 | 60 | 62 | 64 | 66 | 68 | 70 | 72 | 74 | 76 |

Page 20: Count by 3s

99.

| 11 | 14 | 17 | 20 | 23 | 26 | 29 | 32 | 35 | 38 |

100.

| 33 | 36 | 39 | 42 | 45 | 48 | 51 | 54 | 57 | 60 |

101.

| 89 | 92 | 95 | 98 | 101 | 104 | 107 | 110 | 113 | 116 |

102.

| 3 | 6 | 9 | 12 | 15 | 18 | 21 | 24 | 27 | 30 |

103.

| 80 | 83 | 86 | 89 | 92 | 95 | 98 | 101 | 104 | 107 |

104.

| 92 | 95 | **98** | 101 | 104 | 107 | 110 | 113 | 116 | 119 |

105.

| 25 | **28** | 31 | 34 | 37 | 40 | 43 | 46 | 49 | 52 |

106.

| 88 | 91 | 94 | 97 | 100 | **103** | 106 | 109 | 112 | 115 |

107.

| 63 | 66 | 69 | **72** | 75 | 78 | 81 | 84 | 87 | 90 |

108.

| 21 | **24** | 27 | 30 | 33 | 36 | 39 | 42 | 45 | 48 |

109.

| 42 | 45 | **48** | 51 | 54 | 57 | 60 | 63 | 66 | 69 |

110.

| 29 | 32 | 35 | 38 | 41 | 44 | 47 | **50** | 53 | 56 |

111.

| 60 | 63 | 66 | 69 | 72 | **75** | 78 | 81 | 84 | 87 |

112.

| 67 | 70 | 73 | 76 | 79 | 82 | 85 | **88** | 91 | 94 |

113.

| 26 | 29 | 32 | 35 | 38 | 41 | **44** | 47 | 50 | 53 |

114.

| 18 | 21 | 24 | 27 | 30 | 33 | 36 | **39** | 42 | 45 |

115.

| 62 | 65 | **68** | 71 | 74 | 77 | 80 | 83 | 86 | 89 |

116.

| 59 | **62** | 65 | 68 | 71 | 74 | 77 | 80 | 83 | 86 |

117.

| 1 | 4 | 7 | 10 | 13 | 16 | 19 | **22** | 25 | 28 |

118.

| 91 | 94 | 97 | 100 | 103 | 106 | 109 | 112 | **115** | 118 |

119.

| 30 | 33 | 36 | 39 | 42 | **45** | 48 | 51 | 54 | 57 |

120.

| 45 | 48 | 51 | 54 | 57 | 60 | **63** | 66 | 69 | 72 |

121.

| 6 | 9 | 12 | 15 | **18** | 21 | 24 | 27 | 30 | 33 |

122.

| 77 | 80 | 83 | 86 | 89 | 92 | 95 | 98 | 101 | **104** |

123.

| 51 | 54 | 57 | 60 | 63 | **66** | 69 | 72 | 75 | 78 |

124.

| 8 | **11** | 14 | 17 | 20 | 23 | 26 | 29 | 32 | 35 |

125.

| 57 | 60 | 63 | 66 | 69 | **72** | 75 | 78 | 81 | 84 |

126.

| 34 | 37 | 40 | 43 | 46 | 49 | 52 | 55 | **58** | 61 |

127.

| 17 | 20 | 23 | 26 | 29 | 32 | 35 | 38 | 41 | 44 |

Page 26: Compare the Numbers

128. <   129. <   130. >   131. <   132. >   133. <   134. <   135. <

136. >   137. >   138. <   139. <   140. <   141. >   142. >   143. <

144. >   145. >   146. >   147. <   148. <   149. >   150. >   151. <

152. <   153. >   154. <   155. >   156. >   157. >   158. <   159. <

160. >   161. <   162. <   163. <   164. <   165. <   166. <   167. >

168. >   169. <   170. >   171. <   172. <   173. <   174. >   175. <

176. >   177. <   178. >   179. >   180. <   181. <   182. >   183. <

184. >   185. >   186. >   187. <   188. >   189. <   190. <   191. <

192. <   193. <   194. <   195. >   196. <   197. <   198. >   199. >

200. <   201. >   202. >   203. <   204. <   205. >   206. <   207. >

208. <   209. <   210. >   211. >   212. >   213. <   214. >   215. <

216. <   217. >   218. >   219. >   220. >   221. <

Page 32: Circle the Numbers

222. 80   223. (100)   224. (25)   225. (1)   226. 70   227. 24   228. 21
     41   (22)   (74)   20   (91)   73   73
      3   56   47   75   (43)   34   15
    (88)   51   48   49   56   (97)   (92)
     (1)   49   40   (98)   88   (12)   (1)

229. (94) 75 17 (9) 62
230. 30 (27) 47 (77) 36
231. (23) 47 25 45 (81)
232. 39 28 (89) 41 (11)
233. 51 60 33 (14) (77)
234. 49 23 (54) 38 (5)
235. (2) 32 (82) 48 46

236. 27 (4) 67 (88) 69
237. 43 44 (67) (20) 65
238. 77 49 (89) (16) 73
239. (94) 84 75 82 (51)
240. 34 (42) (3) 33 13
241. (8) (73) 10 72 34
242. 91 66 77 (99) (55)

243. 35 61 (2) (73) 68
244. (8) 94 13 49 (100)
245. (1) 34 38 (65) 12
246. 18 58 (1) (98) 13
247. (85) (1) 35 75 62
248. 71 (34) (95) 86 74
249. (12) 72 (91) 62 38

250. 33 (83) (2) 14 43
251. 40 30 (55) 33 (12)
252. (75) 35 45 61 (17)
253. (34) 65 80 (87) 70
254. 35 27 (11) (98) 74
255. (100) (28) 75 89 30
256. 43 77 (27) (79) 36

257. 56 (87) 55 73 (47)
258. (2) 64 88 36 (89)
259. (34) 70 41 47 (92)
260. (4) (92) 6 56 16
261. 69 41 (3) (81) 45
262. (83) 32 59 (18) 81
263. 78 26 (14) 15 (89)

264. 26
64
(24)
63
(85)

265. (66)
58
(34)
42
38

266. 40
(85)
(23)
73
80

267. 65
72
(86)
(33)
54

268. 66
58
(81)
(57)
77

269. 71
(52)
(89)
63
70

270. 67
(91)
78
(16)
81

271. (93)
69
(54)
84
76

272. 45
47
(3)
46
(93)

273. 75
(95)
10
(2)
14

274. (7)
40
(81)
62
23

275. 68
84
67
(87)
(15)

276. (14)
69
72
(73)
71

277. 49
(8)
93
88
(97)

278. 19
(2)
(58)
9
20

279. 55
36
65
(3)
(76)

280. 43
(88)
50
63
(28)

281. 10
17
(94)
13
(2)

282. 68
70
62
(76)
(31)

283. 75
44
67
(88)
(17)

284. (15)
18
(89)
38
24

285. (53)
3
14
48
(2)

286. (84)
39
72
82
(22)

287. (10)
44
39
(91)
14

288. 80
78
(95)
52
(32)

289. (96)
33
45
(24)
61

290. (21)
36
(89)
26
74

291. (33)
75
(90)
87
64

292. 91
99
(62)
(100)
84

293. 32
91
(95)
54
(22)

294. 32
(6)
(76)
75
37

295. 37
23
(38)
(6)
29

296. (20)
59
(90)
88
82

297. 48
51
46
(9)
(90)

298. 35
(54)
53
28
(23)

299. 81
17
95
68
1

300. 6
39
91
3
29

301. 16
60
15
89
37

302. 10
38
84
58
45

303. 33
10
74
19
36

304. 82
45
87
65
79

305. 53
49
52
56
21

306. 29
70
6
23
81

307. 68
88
60
66
89

308. 37
58
72
80
98

309. 71
95
83
91
72

310. 43
76
32
19
61

311. 53
26
16
51
64

312. 11
63
33
17
82

313. 68
78
36
64
65

314. 22
15
54
48
46

315. 88
15
85
90
8

316. 59
66
62
85
79

317. 53
38
87
63
29

318. 42
72
9
3
78

319. 74
25
56
99
30

320. 93
60
20
26
50

Page 43: Missing Numbers

321. 29
322. 85 87
323. 74
324. 41
325. 44

326. 46
327. 49
328. 29
329. 92 94
330. 36

331. 52
332. 51 53
333. 72 74
334. 60
335. 61

336. 99
337. 36
338. 51
339. 54
340. 91

341. 2
342. 68
343. 33 35
344. 77
345. 72

346. 3	347. 86	348. 101	349. 74	350. 3
351. 80 82	352. 67	353. 8	354. 68	355. 89
356. 78	357. 84	358. 23	359. 40 42	360. 39
361. 88	362. 17 19	363. 16	364. 63	365. 58
366. 13	367. 11	368. 80	369. 91	370. 6 8
371. 31 33	372. 24	373. 4	374. 82	375. 84
376. 79	377. 23	378. 40	379. 14	380. 37
381. 42	382. 69	383. 35	384. 27	385. 64
386. 96	387. 10	388. 39	389. 10	390. 54
391. 46	392. 62	393. 57 59	394. 8 10	395. 30
396. 99 101	397. 83 85	398. 31	399. 57	400. 8
401. 70	402. 7	403. 70	404. 88	405. 14
406. 79 81	407. 48 50	408. 68 70	409. 71 73	410. 6
411. 44	412. 16 18	413. 37	414. 16	